1

AVENUES
English Grammar

Lynne Gaetz

PEARSON
Longman

5757 CYPIHOT STREET, SAINT-LAURENT (QUÉBEC) CANADA H4S 1R3
TELEPHONE: 1 800 263-3678 EXT. 232   FAX: 1 866 334-0448
infoesl@erpi.com   www.longman-esl.ca

Managing Editor
Sharnee Chait

Project Editor
Linda Barton

Proofreader
Lynn-Marie Holland

Photo Research and Permissions
Pierre-Richard Bernier

Art Director
Hélène Cousineau

Graphic Design Coordinator
Lyse LeBlanc

Graphic Design and Layout
Interscript

Illustrations
Louise Catherine Bergeron

Cover Design
Frédérique Bouvier

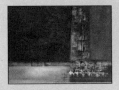

Cover Artwork
Pietro Adamo. *Citta Series*, 2008. Mixed media on canvas, 36 x 48 inches. Courtesy of Progressive Fine Art and Galerie Beauchamp. © 2011 Pietro Adamo.

© 2011 PEARSON Longman Published and distributed by
ÉDITIONS DU RENOUVEAU PÉDAGOGIQUE INC.

Registration of copyright – Bibliothèque et Archives nationales du Québec, 2011
Registration of copyright – Library and Archives Canada, 2011

Printed in Canada
ISBN 978-2-7613-3839-4

56789 II 17 16 15 14
133839 ABCD   ENV94

Acknowledgements

Many people helped produce what you hold in your hands. I would like to express sincere thanks to

- Sharnee Chait for her valuable expertise;
- Linda Barton for her patience and insight while editing this book;
- Julie Hough for her enthusiasm which helped ignite this project;
- My students at Collège Lionel-Groulx for their insightful feedback;
- Diego Pelaez for his valuable contributions to this manuscript and the Companion Website;
- Geneviève Beaulieu for the creative layout.

Finally, I dedicate this to my husband Octavio and to my children Diego and Rebeka.

This book is printed on paper made in Québec from 100% post-consumer recycled materials, processed chlorine-free, certified Eco-Logo, and manufactured using biogas energy.

TABLE OF CONTENTS

UNIT 1 Pronouns

Preview

WHAT ARE PRONOUNS?

Pronouns are words that replace nouns (people, places, or things), other pronouns, and phrases. Use pronouns to avoid repeating nouns.

Martin has an unusual job. ~~Martin~~ designs roller coasters.

(*He* written above crossed-out *Martin*)

PRONOUN CROSSWORD

Complete the following crossword with a partner. Discuss your answers.

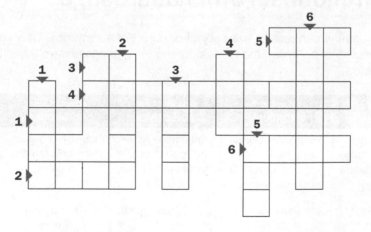

Across

1 ▶ Did you meet Dan? ... is nice.
2 ▶ You have a car. Is that ... car?
3 ▶ This is a great day because ... is sunny.
4 ▶ Some people live by ....
5 ▶ The car lost ... wheel on the highway.
6 ▶ The dog belongs to Adam and me. It is ...

Down

1 ▶ Fans dance when ... hear Lady Gaga songs.
2 ▶ The musicians carry ... own instruments.
3 ▶ The iPod belongs to me. It is ...
4 ▶ Lady Gaga writes ... own songs.
5 ▶ We should ask ... friends for help.
6 ▶ The car belongs to Jake and Liz. It is ...

Reading and Listening

IDENTIFY PRONOUNS

Fill in the blanks with the appropriate pronouns and possessive adjectives. On the Companion Website, listen to an audio recording of the reading. You can correct your answers.

> **EXAMPLE:** Do _you_ know Lady Gaga?

1. Stefani Germanotta learned to play the piano when _____ was four.

2. Ten years later, _____ wrote a song and performed _____ in a New York City club. **3.** Then Germanotta wrote music for other performers.

4. Britney Spears and New Kids on the Block performed _____ songs.

5. In 2006, Germanotta became Lady Gaga, and she developed _____ own style. **6.** A year later, Rapper Akon added Gaga to _____ record label.

7. In 2008, Gaga released the song "Poker Face," and _____ became an international hit. **8.** People listened to the song on _____ iPods.

9. Gaga appreciates her fans and often thanks _____. **10.** Recently, Gaga said, "Some women follow a man and others follow _____ dreams."

Pronouns: Forms and Usage

Pronouns can replace the subject or object of a sentence. They can also indicate possession. Review the types of pronouns and possessive adjectives in the table below.

	SUBJECT PRONOUNS	OBJECT PRONOUNS	POSSESSIVE ADJECTIVES	POSSESSIVE PRONOUNS	REFLEXIVE PRONOUNS
	replace the subject and are generally followed by a verb.	replace the object and are usually found after a verb or preposition.	describe a noun and appear before the noun that they describe.	indicate possession and replace a noun.	reflect back on the subject.
	She lives alone.	I saw **him** yesterday.	That is **our** house.	That house is **ours**.	The child can feed **herself**.
Singular	I you he she it	me you him her it	my your his her its	mine yours his hers –	myself yourself himself herself itself
Plural	we you they	us you them	our your their	ours yours theirs	ourselves yourselves themselves

Practice

SUBJECT AND OBJECT PRONOUNS

A **subject pronoun** performs the action and is usually followed by a verb. An **object pronoun** replaces an object and is usually found after a verb or preposition.

subject   object

She   ***them***

<u>Officer Kate Rowan</u> arrested <u>the bank robbers</u>.

EXERCISE 1 SUBJECT AND OBJECT PRONOUNS

Replace the underlined words with a subject or object pronoun.

She

EXAMPLE: Alison lives alone. <u>Alison</u> pays the rent every month.

1. Alison and her boyfriend Steve share an apartment. <u>The apartment</u> is very small. <u>Alison and Steve</u> are not compatible. Steve spends many hours on the computer. <u>The computer</u> has a lot of games. <u>Steve</u> downloads <u>the games</u> from the Internet. Alison often complains because Steve doesn't spend enough time with <u>Alison</u>.

2. Alison has a very bad habit. <u>Alison</u> bites her nails. <u>Her nails</u> are short and fragile. She needs to stop biting <u>her nails</u>.

3. I know Steve because I work with <u>Steve</u>. <u>Steve and I</u> work in a customer service department. Every day, people complain to <u>Steve and I</u> about certain products.

TIP

Avoid Double Subjects

Do not to repeat the subject with the pronoun form. (A subject pronoun <u>replaces</u> the subject.)

Mr. Spenser ~~he~~ is friendly.

EXERCISE 2 AVOID DOUBLE SUBJECTS

Cross out the five repeated subjects in the following paragraph.

    EXAMPLE: My apartment *it* is really noisy.

My new apartment has large windows. The windows they face a large park.
The park it is full of trees, and there is a small lake near the back of the park.
Often, early in the morning, my roommate and I we go for a walk in the park.
The exercise it is good for us. Then my roommate he takes a bus to work, and
I walk to my college.

POSSESSIVE ADJECTIVES AND POSSESSIVE PRONOUNS

Possessive adjectives describe a noun and appear before the noun that they
describe.

Possessive pronouns replace the possessive adjective and noun.

possessive adjective	possessive pronoun
*Anne and Rick lost **their** passport.*	*Did you lose **yours**?*

EXERCISE 3 POSSESSIVE ADJECTIVES AND POSSESSIVE PRONOUNS

Fill in the blanks with the correct possessive adjectives and possessive pronouns.

Whose cup is it?

EXAMPLE:

I have a cup.

It is _____my_____ cup.

It is _____mine_____ .

3. He has a cup.

   That is _____ cup.

   That is _____ .

1. You have a cup.

   That is _____ cup.

   That is _____ .

4. We have cups.

   These are _____ cups.

   These are _____ .

2. She has a cup.

   That is _____ cup.

   That is _____ .

5. They have cups.

   Those are _____ cups.

   Those are _____ .

CHOOSING *HIS*, *HER*, OR *ITS*

To choose the correct possessive adjective, think about the possessor, not the object that is possessed.

If something belongs to a female, use **her**.

If something belongs to a male, use **his**.

If something belongs to an object, use **its**.

her brother
her father
her house

his car
his mother
his daughter

its muffler
its wheels
its windshield

EXERCISE 4 POSSESSIVE ADJECTIVES

Fill in the blanks with the correct possessive adjectives.

EXAMPLE: Pierre and Gloria have a nice apartment. That is _their_ apartment.

1. Pierre and Gloria have an apartment, and they own many books. Those are _____ books. Also, those images on the wall are _____ pictures.

2. Look at Gloria. That is _____ green dress, and those are _____ earrings. _____ blond hair is very short. She owns an old phone. _____ antique phone is on the floor near _____ feet.

3. Pierre is beside Gloria. Pierre is _____ boyfriend. Pierre has sunglasses. _____ sunglasses are on _____ head. Also, those are _____ black pants. Gloria is _____ girlfriend.

4. Pierre is close to _____ parents. They live nearby. _____ house is two blocks away from Gloria and Pierre's apartment.

Write the correct possessive adjectives or possessive pronouns in the spaces provided. Choose from the words in parentheses.

EXAMPLE: (her / hers) Julie lives with <u>her</u> family.

1. (her / hers) Julie has a passion for old movies. She has a large collection, and she keeps _____ favorite DVDs in a special closet. _____ TV is in her bedroom. I like my DVDs, but I don't like _____.

2. (our / ours) My brother and I usually watch action movies on _____ TV. Last weekend, Julie's television was broken, but _____ worked, so Julie wanted to watch a movie with us. She wanted to watch a romance movie, but we wanted to watch _____ action movie. Finally, Julie went back to her apartment, and we stayed in _____.

3. (their / theirs) Mr. and Mrs. Randall collect DVDs. _____ collection consists mainly of horror movies. I rarely watch _____ movies. I like my movie collection, but I don't like _____.

COMMONLY CONFUSED WORDS

Do not confuse the following pronouns with similar sounding words.

His is a possessive adjective.   *Carl works with **his** brother.*
Is is a form of the verb *be*.   *He **is** a hard worker.*
He's means *he is*.   ***He's** busy today.*

Its is a possessive adjective.   *The company has **its** annual party in May.*
It's is the contraction of *it is*.   ***It's** a very nice party.*

Your is a possessive adjective.   ***Your** painting is beautiful.*
You're is the contraction of *you are*.   ***You're** a great friend.*

Their is a possessive adjective.   ***Their** house is blue.*
They're is the contraction of *they are*.   ***They're** going to move.*
There indicates that something exists.   ***There** are many bedrooms in the house.*

In each sentence, underline the correct word in parentheses. Note that X means nothing is needed.

EXAMPLE: Jane watched the movie with (his / <u>her</u>) boyfriend.

1. Jason Reitman (he / X) is a movie director. He was born in Montreal in 1977. He directed *Juno* and *Up in the Air*. (His / Her / Is) father is also a well-known director. Ivan Reitman directed (is / his / her) movies in both Canada and the United States. Jason Reitman once said, "(My / Mine) father influenced (my / me)."

2. Both Ivan and Jason Reitman read a lot of scripts. (There / They're / Their) really busy people. They are serious about (there / they're / their) work.

3. Last night, my sister and I watched *Up in the Air* on (ours / our) family computer. The computer is new, and (it's / its / X) screen is very large. I loved the movie. (It's / Its) really interesting.

4. (Ours / Our) friends came and brought Ivan Reitman's old movie *Ghostbusters*. We watched (their / theirs / X) movie, and they watched (our / ours). Later, we talked about the movies of Jason Reitman. They listened to (our / ours) opinions and we listened to (their / theirs).

5. My sister (she / X) turned to me and said, "I know what (you're / your) thinking. (You're / Your / Yours) opinion is clear. You like *Up in the Air* more than *Ghostbusters*."

REFLEXIVE PRONOUNS

Reflexive pronouns are used when the subject doing the action and the object receiving the action are the same person or thing.

*The small <u>boy</u> dressed **himself**.*

Remember that *you* has both singular and plural reflexive pronouns.
   yourself (one person: you)
   yourselves (more than one person: you and others)

The expression "by oneself" means "alone."
   *I can do it by **myself**.*

EXERCISE 7 REFLEXIVE PRONOUNS

Write the correct reflexive pronouns in the blanks.

   EXAMPLE: I often talk to _myself_.

1. One day, while I was walking in the woods with my friend Jonathan, he hurt _____. He twisted his knee. Nobody was near us. We were by _____.

2. Suddenly, a girl arrived. She was not with anybody else. She was by _____. She helped Jonathan. Then she turned to me and said, "Go get some help. Go by _____. I will stay here with Jonathan."

3. I could not use my cellphone because there were no towers nearby, so I walked to get some help. Jonathan and the girl stayed in the woods by _____.

To hear the correct pronunciation of pronouns and to try additional exercises, visit the Companion Website.

4. About fifteen minutes later, I was able to get cellphone reception, and I called for help. Then as I was walking back to Jonathan, I cut _____ on a piece of glass.

TIP

Pronoun Errors

Always capitalize the first person pronoun *I*. Don't use *hisself* or *theirselves*. They are incorrect ways to say *himself* and *themselves*.

>   **I**   **themselves**
> *Sometimes ~~i~~ visit the Smiths. Yesterday, they helped ~~theirselves~~ to the food.*
>
>   **himself**
> *Jeff ate by ~~hisself~~.*

EXERCISE 8 IDENTIFY ERRORS

Each sentence contains one or two errors involving a pronoun or a commonly confused word. Correct the errors.

                              herself
EXAMPLE: My aunt works by <u>himself</u>.

1. Uncle Raymond influences me because his so talented.

2. Raymond his a passionate photographer.

3. Is cameras are really expensive.

4. In his photography studio, he works by hisself.

5. When i have time, i visit my uncle's studio.

6. If your looking for a great photographer, you should visit my uncle.

7. Its difficult to find a better photographer.

8. Maybe you need a photographer for you're wedding.

9. My friends take photos by theirselves.

10. Uncle Raymond he is successful, and i want to be like him.

EXERCISE 9 MIXED PRONOUNS

Fill in the blanks with the correct pronoun or possessive adjective.

> EXAMPLE: Tara Blue has a great dancing style, and _her_ performances are
> very good.

1. Tara Blue has a very strong passion. _____ is a dancer.

   _____ created the Blue Collar Dance Company by _____.

   _____ is a modern dance company.

2. Tara learned to dance as a child. Then _____ studied dance in

   Montreal. In 2005, she returned to _____ hometown of Calgary.

   _____ dance company is quite successful.

3. People pay to see Tara dance. Usually,

   _____ love Tara's performances.

   Sometimes, admirers donate some of

   _____ money to the dance company.

4. Mr. Vince Arnaud is a choreographer.

   _____ creates original and vibrant

   dances. Dancers love _____ style, and

   they respect _____.

5. Mr. Arnaud always creates by _____. Then

   he shows _____ ideas to the dancers.

CHOOSING THE CORRECT PRONOUN

Be careful when there is more than one subject or object. When a pronoun is
the **subject** of a sentence, use the subject form. When it is the **object**, use the
object form.

> subject   object
> _My brother and **I** love to dance. Our parents watch <u>my sister and **me**</u>._

If you are not sure which form to use, try saying the sentence with just one
pronoun.

> _The teacher helped Edward and (I or me)._

Possible choices: _The teacher helped **I**. The teacher helped **me**._
Correct answer: _The teacher helped Edward and **me**._

EXERCISE 10 MIXED PRONOUNS

In each sentence, underline the appropriate word in parentheses.

> EXAMPLE: What is (<u>your</u> / yours) favourite show?

1. For his last show, Mr. Arnaud worked with a violinist and a bass player. He paid (them / themselves) a lot of money. The musicians sat beside the stage and they played (their / theirs) instruments.

2. After the final show, there was a party with a large buffet. The performers helped (theirselves / themselves / yourselves) to the food. Then the dancers received (their / theirs) salaries, and the two musicians also received (their / theirs).

3. The dancers perform in an art-deco building. (He / She / It) is an old building. I rent an apartment in the same building. My friend Fernando lives with (my / me / mine). (Our / Ours) apartment is very small, but it is nice. I think it is nicer than (your / yours).

4. Fernando and (I / me) are musicians. Fernando is talented, and (he / him) plays the drums. I play the flute. Sometimes (him and me / he and I) argue about music. When he practises, I ignore (his / him / himself). I do (my / mine) work, and he does (his / him). Sometimes our neighbours complain to Fernando and (I / me). They ask (we / us) to be quiet.

↻ UNIT Review

Answer the following questions. If you don't know an answer, go back and review the appropriate section.

1. Underline and correct the pronoun errors in the following sentences. Explain why each sentence is incorrect.

   a) Kelsey she is a really hard worker. _____

   Reason: _____

   b) My sister moved in with his boyfriend. _____

   Reason: _____

   c) We put ours dogs outside. _____

   Reason: _____

2. Fill in the missing object pronouns below.

   a) I ___me___   c) he _____   e) it _____   g) they _____

   b) you _____   d) she _____   f) we _____

3. Correct one pronoun spelling error in each sentence. Underline the error and then make the correction.

   a) The boys sometimes help theirselfs to food. _____

   b) Look at the baby! He can feed hisself now. _____

   c) The Johnsons leave there doors unlocked. _____

Final Review

Underline the correct word in parentheses.

   EXAMPLE: My boyfriend bought (<u>me</u> / mine / my) a gift.

1. My neighbours, Julie and Marie, own a bakery, and I work with (they / their / themselves / them).

2. They influence (me / mine / my) a lot.

3. (It's / She's / Its) a very successful business because Julie and Marie are passionate cooks.

4. Sometimes, I work with another part-time worker named Jonathan. We bake the cakes and muffins. We often work by (ourself / ourselves / theirselves).

5. Occasionally we make mistakes, and we get to eat (our / ours / us) mistakes.

6. At first, I loved to eat a lot of muffins, but now I do not like to eat (they / theirs / them) as often. I gained too much weight!

7. Jonathan is funny, so I like to work with (he / his / him).

8. At times, when the store is really quiet, Jonathan works by (hisself / himself / herself).

9. Mr. and Mrs. Lee own a competing bakery. (Their / Theirs / Them) customers are very loyal.

10. The Lees' cakes are tasty, but so are (our / ours).

11. We sell to our customers, and they sell to (their / theirs).

12. Clients can phone (us / our / ourselves) and make an order.

13. Julie uses (her / hers) special recipes to make birthday cakes.

14. Each cake has (it's / its / his) own particular design.

15. Last year, our bosses gave bonuses to Jonathan and (I / me).

WRITING   On a separate piece of paper, write a paragraph about someone who influences you. Describe that person's unique qualities and actions. After you finish writing, underline the pronouns.

Simple Present

Preview

WHAT IS THE SIMPLE PRESENT?

The **simple present** indicates general truths, facts, habitual actions, and customs.

Facts	*Birds **have** wings.*
Habits/Routines	*Alicia **shops** every Saturday.*
Customs	*Devout Muslims **fast** during Ramadan.*

FACTS AND QUESTIONS

Write five facts about yourself and your family. You can write things such as your nickname, age, workplace, hobby, or any other interesting detail. Exchange books with your partner. He or she must then write the question for each fact. Review the example.

Fact: I am in sciences.

Question: What program are you in?

1. Fact: _____

   Question: _____

2. Fact: _____

   Question: _____

3. Fact: _____

   Question: _____

4. Fact: _____

   Question: _____

5. Fact: _____

   Question: _____

Reading and Listening

IDENTIFY SIMPLE PRESENT VERBS

Fill in the blanks with the appropriate simple present verb form. You can choose from the words below. Use affirmative and negative forms. On the Companion Website, listen to an audio recording of the reading. You can correct your answers.

be	deliver	lift	treat	work
bring	keep	need	transfer	

1. Zac Renfrew _____ a nurse. **2.** He _____ in a large hospital. **3.** Every weekend, he _____ patients in the emergency room. **4.** According to Zac, a nurse _____ both physical and emotional strength. **5.** Often, nurses _____ patients who fall. **6.** Nurses _____ patients from stretchers to beds or from beds to wheelchairs. **7.** The job of a nurse _____ also very stressful emotionally. **8.** Zac _____ bad news to patients and their families. **9.** To survive, Zac _____ his work home with him. **10.** He _____ his work separate from his private life.

Simple Present: Forms and Usage

The simple present indicates general truths, facts, habitual actions, and customs.

Kate **works** three days a week.

(past) ← Kate **works**. Kate **works**. Kate **works**. → (future)

Monday	Tuesday	Wednesday	Thursday	Friday
5th	6th	7th	8th	9th

Key Words: always, frequently, generally, never, occasionally, often, rarely, seldom, sometimes, usually

AFFIRMATIVE, QUESTION, AND NEGATIVE FORMS

All Verbs Except *Be*

AFFIRMATIVE FORM		QUESTION FORM (Add *do* or *does*.)			NEGATIVE FORM (Add *do not* or *does not*.)	
I	**know**.	**Do**	I	**know**?	I	**do not know**. (don't)
She He It	**knows**.	**Does**	she he it	**know**?	She He It	**does not know**. (doesn't)
You We They	**know**.	**Do**	you we they	**know**?	You We They	**do not know**. (don't)

Be

AFFIRMATIVE FORM		QUESTION FORM (Move *be*.)		NEGATIVE FORM (Add *not*.)	
I	**am**.	**Am**	I	I	**am not**.
She He It	**is**.	**Is**	she? he? it?	She He It	**is not**. (isn't)
You We They	**are**.	**Are**	you? we? they?	You We They	**are not**. (aren't)

When to Use *Be*

Name, age, gender	How old **is** Garret? He **is** twenty. (Incorrect: He ~~has~~ twenty.)
Emotions	He **is** afraid / scared. They **are** upset / tired / happy.
Size and shape	She **is** 165 cm tall. The building **is** big / tall / heavy / square.
Hunger, thirst	**Are** you thirsty? I **am** hungry. (Incorrect: I ~~have~~ hungry.)
Temperature, time	It **is** 20 degrees Celsius. What time **is** it? It **is** 4:30 a.m.

THERE + BE

There is means that something exists. *There* is a "false" subject, and the real subject follows the verb *be*. (Note that *there is* means *il y a* in French or *hay* in Spanish.)

There is one person or thing   **There is** <u>a health clinic</u> downtown.
There are two or more people or things   **There are** <u>many people</u> in the clinic.

Question Form: Move the verb *be* before *there*.

Is there a health clinic? **Are** there many people?

Practice

EXERCISE 1 *BE AND HAVE*

Fill in the blanks with the correct form of *be* and *have*.

    is   am   are   have   has

    EXAMPLE: Lauren Wells <u>is</u> a medical resident.

1.   Medical residents _____ very demanding work. In many places, they

    _____ an eighty-hour work week. Lauren Wells _____

    twenty-four years old, and she _____ a medical student. She

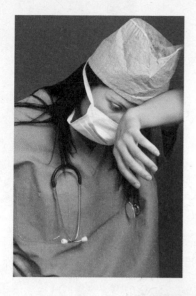

_____ a very demanding schedule. Every day, Lauren _____ in a hospital. She doesn't have breaks, so when she _____ hungry, she waits until the ward is quiet. Then she _____ a break.

2. I _____ Lauren's friend, and I worry about her. Sometimes, she works for twenty hours, and she _____ extremely tired. She _____ a tiny person, and she doesn't eat well. Her friends also _____ some concerns. Some medical students _____ upset about their long workdays. Unfortunately, the Canadian government _____ very quiet about the issue.

EXERCISE 2 *BE*: NEGATIVE AND QUESTION FORMS

PART A

Make the verbs in the sentences negative. Use the contracted form.

EXAMPLE: Alex **is** a weightlifter.   isn't

1. Some people **are** healthy.   _____

2. Alex **is** in great condition.   _____

3. However, his parents **are** lazy.   _____

4. His father **is** a couch potato.   _____

5. Regular exercise **is** important.   _____

PART B

Write a yes/no question for each of the following sentences.

EXAMPLE: The gym is open.   Is the gym open?

6. The weights are expensive.

_____

7. The gym is old.

_____

8. The treadmills are loud.

_____

9. The gym is full of people.

_____

10. Alex is in great shape.

_____

There is/There are

There **is** <u>one item</u>. There **are** <u>two or more items</u>.

In questions, move *be* before *there*.

Is *there a shirt?*   **Are** *there three plates?*

EXERCISE 3 THERE IS/THERE ARE

PART A

Describe what items are in the shopping cart. Use *There is* or *There are*. Also use the following expressions: *a pair of/a package of*.

> **EXAMPLE:** There is a blue shirt and a tie.

1. _____
2. _____
3. _____
4. _____
5. _____
6. _____

PART B

Write three questions about the photo in Part A.

> **EXAMPLE:** Is there a blue shirt and a tie?

8. _____
9. _____
10. _____

SPELLING RULES: ADDING –S OR –ES

- Add –**es** to verbs ending in –*s*, –*sh*, –*ss*, –*ch*, –*o*, or –*x*.

  wish — wish**es**   go — go**es**

- Change –**y** to –**ies** when verbs end in a consonant + –*y*.

  marry — marr**ies**   study — stud**ies**

- Keep the –**y** and add –**s** when the verb ends in a vowel + –*y*.

  play — play**s**   stay — stay**s**

EXERCISE 4 THIRD-PERSON SINGULAR VERBS

In the space, write the third-person singular form of the following verbs.

EXAMPLE: I want. She _wants_ .

1. I study.   She _____.
2. I wash.   He _____.
3. You try.   She _____.
4. I care.   He _____.
5. They stop.   It _____.
6. We go.   It _____.

7. We talk.   He _____.
8. You eat.   She _____.
9. I worry.   She _____.
10. We touch.   He _____.
11. They do.   It _____.
12. You push.   He _____.

SUBJECT-VERB AGREEMENT

If the subject is **one** person, place, or thing (but not *you* or *I*), add –s or –es to the verb.

Person   _Pedro_ **works** in a hospital.

Place   _Canada_ **needs** high-speed trains.

Thing   _The roof_ **leaks**.

If there is **more than one** subject, use the base form of the verb. (The base form is the form you would see in a dictionary. It has no special word ending.)

Pedro and his brother **work** in a hospital.

TIP

Afraid or
Scared?

I am afraid and
I am scared mean
the same thing.

EXERCISE 5 SUBJECT-VERB AGREEMENT

Underline the correct simple present form of the verbs in parentheses.

EXAMPLE: That man (have / <u>has</u>) large muscles.

1. Humans and other creatures (have / has) defence mechanisms. Humans (fight / fights) with their fists, their legs, and their teeth. Some animals (have / has) very unique ways to defend themselves.

2. Skunks (is / are) very clever creatures. The innocent-looking animal (have / has) a white stripe down its back, and it (appear / appears) cute and defenceless. But all skunks (possess / possesses) a powerful weapon. They (spray / sprays) their enemies with a disgusting liquid. The offensive spray even (repel / repels) bears and other large mammals.

3. When a skunk (feel / feels) afraid, it (turn / turns) away from its enemy. It (place / places) its feet firmly on the ground. Then the skunk (look / looks) over its shoulder, and it (arch / arches) its back. It (aim / aims) and (shoot / shoots). According to Desmond Morris, in *Animal Watching*, "a skunk (swing / swings) its body from side to side, like a machine gunner. This action (give / gives) the spray a wider range—an arch of about forty-five degrees."

SPECIAL SUBJECTS

Indefinite pronouns beginning with *every-, some-, any-,* and *no-* are considered singular. To help you remember this rule, notice that the last part of each word is singular.

everybody	everyone	everything	everywhere
somebody	someone	something	somewhere
nobody	no one	nothing	nowhere

Everybody **wants** *some coffee, but nobody* **has** *any money.*

Sometimes a **gerund** (*–ing* form of the verb) is the subject of a sentence. The subject is considered third-person singular, so you must add *–s* or *–es* to the verb.

Animal training **requires** *patience.*

EXERCISE 6 SUBJECT-VERB AGREEMENT

Underline the correct simple present form of the verbs in parentheses.

 EXAMPLE: People (<u>shop</u> / shops) for several reasons.

1. Everybody (need / needs) affection.

2. Nobody (want / wants) to be ignored.

3. Most people (have / has) companions.

4. Usually, nobody (choose / chooses) to be alone forever.

5. Most animal species (spend / spends) time in their social groups.

6. Everyone (have / has) one mate or a series of mates.

7. Porcupines, however, (are / is) extremely choosy.

8. A female porcupine (ignore / ignores) the advances of males.

9. She only (want / wants) attention from a male for about twelve hours per year.

10. Almost everybody (agree / agrees) that love and companionship are important.

NEGATIVE FORMS

To form negative simple present verbs, place *do* or *does* and the word *not* between the subject and the verb.

We **do** <u>**not**</u> **have** *a family doctor.*   (contraction: **don't have**)
Kate **does** <u>**not**</u> **work** *every day.*   (contraction: **doesn't work**)

Exception: When the main verb is *be* (*is, am, are*), just add *not*.

The song **is** <u>**not**</u> *popular.*   (contraction: **isn't**)
The singers **are** <u>**not**</u> *loud.*   (contraction: **aren't**)

EXERCISE 7 NEGATIVE FORMS

Add –s or –es to the italicized verbs, if necessary. Then write the contracted negative form of each verb.

Contracted Negative Form

EXAMPLE: Singing improve **_s_** the health.   <u>doesn't improve</u>

1. Jasim Asali *sing*____ every day.   _____

2. Jasim write____ songs.   _____

3. Jasim *teach*____ singing to seniors.   _____

4. They *enjoy*____ the activity.   _____

5. They *do*____ the activity in a nursing home.   _____

6. Jasim *play*____ the piano every evening.   _____

QUESTION FORMS

Add an auxiliary (*do* or *does*) before the subject. Note that the subject must agree with the auxiliary. The main verb is in the base form.

He likes rap music.

                                           base form

Does he <u>like</u> rap music?

Exception: *Be* doesn't need an auxiliary verb. In question forms, just place *be* (*is, am*, or *are*) before the subject.

New iPads are very expensive.   **Are** new <u>iPads</u> very expensive?

TIP

When the Main Verb Is *Do*

Do is both a verb and an auxiliary. When the main verb is *do* or *does*, you must still add an auxiliary to question and negative forms.

                                                    auxiliary   verb

She does her homework.   *She **does** not **do** her homework.*

EXERCISE 8 QUESTION FORMS

PART A

Write *do, does, is, am*, or *are* in the spaces below.

EXAMPLES: <u>Does</u> it have a battery? <u>Are</u> they useful?

1. _____ placebos help people?

2. _____ you feel healthy?

3. _____ some medications dangerous?

4. _____ Wade need sleeping pills?

5. _____ an aspirin safe?

6. _____ the pharmacy give warnings about certain drugs?

PART B

Make negative questions by adding *not* to the auxiliary. Use the contracted form.

EXAMPLE: <u>Don't</u> you visit zoos?

7. _____ that clinic open today?

8. _____ the doctors too busy?

9. _____ your sister have a health problem?

FREQUENCY ADVERBS

Frequency adverbs describe the frequency of an action.

never	rarely	seldom	sometimes occasionally	usually generally	often frequently	always

← 0%　　　　　　　　　　　　　　　　　　　　　100% of the time →

Placement of Mid-Sentence Frequency Adverbs

Place frequency adverbs in the following positions:

– after *be*	*She is **often** tired. He is **rarely** late.*
– before all other simple-tense verbs	*He **rarely** lies. I **sometimes** invent stories.*
– after auxiliary verbs	*She can **always** help us.*
– after the subject in question forms	*Does she **occasionally** lie?*

EXERCISE 9　PLACEMENT OF FREQUENCY ADVERBS

Draw arrows to indicate where the frequency adverbs should be placed in the sentences below.

EXAMPLE: (sometimes) Alan ⌃ takes the bus home from work.

1. (seldom)　　Brad Williams forgets things.
2. (often)　　He remembers trivial events.
3. (usually)　　His memories are correct.
4. (frequently)　　He is faster than a computer.
5. (always)　　He organizes memories better than other people.
6. (sometimes)　　Are his recollections incorrect?
7. (often)　　Does he make a mistake?
8. (occasionally)　　He loses his keys.

EXERCISE 10　IDENTIFY ERRORS

Each sentence below contains one error. Underline and correct the error.

EXAMPLE: What <u>do</u> your brother like to eat?　　does

1. My cousin have health problems.　　_____
2. Do Francis believe in alternative therapies?　　_____
3. He don't want to visit a regular doctor.　　_____

TIP

Showing Agreement

Agree is a regular verb. Don't use *be* to express agreement.

~~I am agree.~~

4. Are you agree with me? _____

5. Why he is so stubborn? _____

6. Francis spend a lot on "miracle" cures. _____

7. Do everybody have the same opinions? _____

8. Francis buys sometimes expensive vitamins. _____

9. Why those pills are so expensive? _____

10. He visits often a naturopath. _____

11. She is'nt very old. _____

12. Francis plan to visit a Mexican clinic. _____

↻ UNIT Review

Answer the following questions. If you don't know an answer, go back and review the appropriate section.

1. When do you put an –s or –es on a verb?

_____

2. Correct the verb error in each sentence, and explain why the sentence is incorrect.

a) They travel sometimes too much. _____

Reason: _____

b) Mr. Smith have an old computer. _____

Reason: _____

c) My laptop don't works very well. _____

Reason: _____

d) Why they spend so much money? _____

Reason: _____

3. Write the contracted negative form of each verb. Then write the question form.

	CONTRACTED NEGATIVE FORM	QUESTION FORM
EXAMPLE: He is old.	isn't	Is he old?
a) They are nice.		
b) They fight a lot.		
c) She sells shoes.		

COMPANION WEB+ Need more practice? Visit the Companion Website to try other simple present exercises and practise pronouncing verbs.

Final Review

PART A

Write the simple present form of the verbs in parentheses below. Then write the contracted negative form in the spaces provided.

EXAMPLE: A dog pedicure (cost) <u>costs</u> a lot.   <u>doesn't cost</u>

1. Kate (have) _____ a poodle and a chihuahua.   _____

2. She (spend) _____ a fortune on her pets.   _____

3. Vaccines (be) _____ expensive.   _____

4. Kate's chihuahua (have) _____ a problem.   _____

5. Her dogs (receive) _____ monthly massages.   _____

PART B

Make yes/no questions out of the following sentences.

    EXAMPLE: Kate lives alone.   <u>Does Kate live alone?</u>

6. The poodle is sad.   _____

7. The dog has a therapist.   _____

8. Dr. Lo charges a high fee.   _____

9. He observes the dog.   _____

10. Some pet owners are silly.   _____

PART C

Correct five errors in the underlined verbs, not including the example. Write *C* above three correct verbs.

    Do
<u>Does</u> you have a pet? Almost everybody <u>love</u> their animals, but some people <u>are</u>

extreme. Kate, a Toronto pet owner, <u>give</u> expensive steak to her dog. Every

morning, she <u>walks</u> past a homeless man, and she <u>don't</u> give him any money.

Yet she <u>buys</u> $200 designer boots for her dog. Why <u>do</u> she spend so much

money on an animal? In Kate's opinion, people <u>has</u> the right to spoil their pets.

 On a separate piece of paper, write six sentences about a friend or family member's health routine. Does that person exercise? Is he or she a couch potato? What does that person eat? After you finish writing, underline your verbs.

UNIT 3

Present Progressive

Preview

WHAT IS THE PRESENT PROGRESSIVE?

Use the **present progressive** when an action is in progress now or for a temporary period of time.

> *Right now, you **are reading** this textbook.*
> *These days, I **am studying** English.*

WHAT ARE THEY DOING?

Work with a partner or a group of students. Under each photo, write what is happening. Choose from the following words.

clap	hug	laugh	snap	stretch	whistle
cry	kick	sip	snore	~~wink~~	whisper

EXAMPLE: He is winking.

Reading and Listening

IDENTIFY PRESENT PROGRESSIVE VERBS

Fill in the blanks with appropriate present progressive verbs (with *be* and an *–ing* verb). Choose from the verbs below. On the Companion Website, listen to an audio recording of the reading. You can correct your answers.

do	examine	look	pay	slide
drive	leave	make	receive	smile

1. Sam just filled his car with gas, and right now he _____ for the gas with his bank card. **2.** The cashier _____ his card carefully.

3. Now, Sam _____ out the window at his girlfriend. **4.** The cashier _____ a very unethical action. **5.** She _____ the card through a second card reader. **6.** The innocent-looking cashier _____ a copy of Sam's bank card data.

7. Now, Sam _____ the gas station. **8.** The cashier _____ because she will earn $100 for Sam's copied data.

9. At this moment, someone else _____ the information and the PIN from Sam's card. **10.** Sam _____ in his car, and he is singing because he is completely unaware of what just happened.

Present Progressive: Forms and Usage

The **present progressive** indicates that an action is happening now.

> Right now, the children **are swimming**.

11 a.m.	Noon	**Right now**	1 p.m.	2 p.m.
		they **are swimming**.		

The **present progressive** also indicates that an action is happening for a present, temporary period of time.

> This week, my sister **is visiting** me.

Last week	**This week**	Next week
	my sister **is visiting** me.	

Key Words: now, currently, presently, at this moment, these days, nowadays, this week, this month

AFFIRMATIVE, QUESTION, AND NEGATIVE FORMS

AFFIRMATIVE FORM		QUESTION FORM (Move *be*.)		NEGATIVE FORM (Add *not*.)	
I	**am** work**ing**.	**Am**	I work**ing**?	I	**am not** work**ing**.
She He It	**is** work**ing**.	**Is**	she he work**ing**? it	She He It	**is not** work**ing**. (isn't working)
You We They	**are** work**ing**.	**Are**	you we work**ing**? they	You We They	**are not** work**ing**. (aren't working)

SPELLING OF –*ING* VERBS

LAST LETTER(S) OF VERB	EXAMPLE	–*ING* FORM	RULE
silent –*e*	smile	smil**ing**	Delete the –*e* and add –*ing*.
–*y*	fly, play	fly**ing**, play**ing**	Just add –*ing*.
–*ie*	lie	l**ying**	Change the –*ie* to –*y* and add –*ing*.
consonant-vowel-consonant	stop	stop**ping**	Double the last letter. **Exception:** words that end in –*x* or –*w* (*snow* ▶ *snowing*).
stressed consonant-vowel-consonant (in verbs of more than one syllable)	re**fer** be**gin**	refe**rring** begi**nning**	Double the last letter when the verb ends in a stressed syllable.
			BUT
	open **hap**pen	open**ing** happen**ing**	If the verb doesn't end in a stressed syllable, just add –*ing*.

NON-PROGRESSIVE VERBS

Some verbs are rarely used in the progressive tenses.

        loves   **wants**
Kara ~~is loving~~ hockey.   She ~~is wanting~~ to compete.

PERCEPTION		PREFERENCE		MENTAL STATE/OPINION		POSSESSION
appear	smell*	dislike	need	believe	recognize	belong
feel*	sound	hate	prefer	forget	remember	have*
hear	resemble	like	want	know	think*	own
see	taste*	love		mean	understand	possess
seem						

* Some verbs have more than one meaning and can be used in the progressive tense. Compare the following: **I think** it is expensive. (Expresses an opinion) / **I am thinking** about it.
He **has** two cars. (Expresses ownership) / He **is having** a bad day.

PRONUNCIATION HELP WITH ONLINE DICTIONARIES

Many dictionaries are available online. On some sites, such as *dictionary.reference. com*, the stressed syllable is indicated in bold, and by clicking on the loudspeaker, you can hear the pronunciation of the word.

    be·gin·ning   ◀))) [bih-gin-ing]

From *dictionary.reference.com*

Practice

SPELL *–ING* **FORMS**
Write the following verbs in their *–ing* form.

       EXAMPLE: sleep   _sleeping_

1. ask   _____
2. shop   _____
3. marry   _____
4. hope   _____
5. write   _____
6. plan   _____
7. open   _____

8. move   _____
9. save   _____
10. try   _____
11. play   _____
12. hit   _____
13. study   _____
14. begin   _____

BE: QUESTION AND NEGATIVE FORMS

Question: The verb *be* acts as an auxiliary and goes before the subject.

Mark is cooking dinner. Why **is Mark cooking** *dinner?*

Negative: Place *not* after the verb *be*.

Mark **is not cooking** *dinner.*

EXERCISE 2 **SENTENCES AND QUESTIONS**
Write sentences describing what the people in the photos are doing. Write an affirmative sentence and a question. (Some photos might require two verbs.)

cover	put on	smile	throw away
~~dream~~	sing	take off	wave

EXAMPLE: _She is dreaming._
            Is she dreaming?

1. _____

2. _____

_____

3. _____

_____

4. _____

_____

5. _____

_____

EXERCISE 3 **PROGRESSIVE VERBS**

The following is a cellphone conversation between two friends. Add in the verbs. Use the affirmative, negative, and question forms of the present progressive.

EXAMPLE: Zaina: Why _are you speaking_ so quickly?

1. Adam: Hi. Right now, what (you, do) _____?

(you, study) _____?

2. Zaina: Oh no, I (study, not) _____.

I (shop) _____ downtown.

3. Adam: Well, right now, I (get) _____ ready for

a job interview. Can you give me your opinion about what I should wear?

4. Zaina: What (you, wear) _____?

(you, put) _____ on your beige suit right now?

5. Adam: No, I (wear, not) _____ a suit. I (plan)

_____ to wear my white shirt and some

jeans.

6. Zaina: Jeans! You can't wear jeans to a job interview. Think! Who

(you, try) _____ to impress?

7. Adam: My jeans are very clean! Also, right now I (put) _____

_____ on my Superman tie.

8. Zaina: No, that is crazy. Listen, right now, I (look) _____

at a very classy tie. It is black and gold. In fact, I (buy) _____

_____ it for you at this moment.

EXERCISE 4 IDENTIFY ERRORS

Correct errors with the present progressive form.

EXAMPLE: The quarterback i̶s̶'̶n̶t̶ isn't holding the ball.

1. Adam is'nt working these days.

2. Right now, he is look for a job.

3. His parents are'nt helping him.

4. They are not pay Adam's rent.

5. Zaina trying to help him.

6. Today, they are'nt relaxing.

7. They searching on Internet job sites.

8. Why is Zaina is complaining?

SIMPLE PRESENT OR PRESENT PROGRESSIVE?

Review the difference between the simple present and the present progressive.

Simple Present	Present Progressive
The action is a fact, habit, or custom.	The action is happening now or for a temporary period of time.

Maya **cycles** *every day.*
Maya **lifts** *weights twice a week.*
Maya **jogs** *every Saturday.*

Right now, Maya **is working**.
These days, she **is writing** *a book.*

EXERCISE 5 SIMPLE PRESENT OR PRESENT PROGRESSIVE

Conjugate the verbs in parentheses to make simple present or present progressive sentences. If the action is a fact or a habit, use the simple present. If the action is happening right now, use the present progressive. After each sentence, write *H* if the verb refers to a habit, *F* if it refers to a fact, or *N* if it refers to an action that is happening now.

> **EXAMPLE:** Look! That man (steal) <u>is stealing</u> your car!   <u>N</u>

1. Justin (exercise) _____ every day.   ____

2. Right now, he (ride) _____ his stationary bike.   ____

3. Justin (spend) _____ a lot of money on sports equipment.   ____

4. At this moment, his friends (use) _____ Justin's equipment.   ____

5. Kyle (run) _____ on Justin's treadmill right now.   ____

6. Look! Alex and Marco (lift) _____ Justin's weights.   ____

7. Justin (have) _____ too much equipment. His apartment is full.   ____

8. Every month, Justin (buy) _____ a new piece of equipment.   ____

TIP

Non-Progressive Verbs

Some verbs are not used in the progressive form because they express a state, preference, perception, or possession. For a list of some non-progressive verbs, see page 25.

> *loves*
> *Pierre is walking in the woods. He ~~is loving~~ nature.*

EXERCISE 6 PROGRESSIVE AND NON-PROGRESSIVE VERBS

Look at each photo and write two sentences using the verbs indicated. One sentence must be in the simple present and one in the present progressive.

EXAMPLE: (watch birds, see a blackbird)

They are **watching** birds.

They **see** a blackbird.

1. (love each other, hold hands)

_____

_____

2. (chew food, need meat)

_____

_____

3. (feel angry, yell into his phone)

_____

_____

4. (fly, see a mouse)

_____

_____

5. (own a video game, play)

_____

_____

TIP

Actually and _Currently_

In English, _actually_ means _really_. It does not mean _at this moment_, _currently_, or _presently_.

       currently
I didn't work last year, but ~~actually~~ I'm working.

EXERCISE 7 CHOOSE THE CORRECT VERB

Complete the following sentences using the simple present or the present progressive.

 EXAMPLE: Samuel (speak) <u> speaks </u> several languages.
     He (speak) <u> is speaking </u> Russian right now.

1. Advertisers (have) _____ many new ways to reach young

people. Companies (want) _____ to sell their products to

youths. Currently, I (watch) _____ a very funny

advertisement on YouTube.

2. The video is called "The Fun Theory." Right now, I (laugh) _____.
At this moment, a man (transform) _____ a staircase in a
subway station. The stairs (resemble) _____ a piano keyboard.

3. A small boy (want) _____ to leave the subway station. Right
now, he (jump) _____ on the piano keys. Look! Other people
(watch) _____ the boy. Now some people (take) _____
_____ the stairs, too. Listen! The stairs (make) _____
_____ music!

4. I (think) _____ that the video is a good advertisement. Viewers
(see) _____ a logo at the end of the video. I really (love)
_____ the video. If you want to see it, search for "The Fun
Theory" on YouTube and watch it!

EXERCISE 8 INFORMATION QUESTIONS

Write questions. The answers to the questions are in bold.

> EXAMPLE: Dan is sleeping **because he is tired**.
> Question: _Why is Dan sleeping?_

1. Sandra is buying hockey tickets **because she loves hockey**.

   Question: _____

2. The game begins **at 10 p.m.**

   Question: _____

3. The tickets cost **$40**.

   Question: _____

4. People are waiting in line **at the stadium**.

   Question: _____

5. The fans are cheering **because the team scored a goal**.

   Question: _____

EXERCISE 9 IDENTIFY ERRORS

Correct ten errors in the underlined verbs. Write *C* above three correct verbs.

flies

> EXAMPLE: Every year, Alana <u>is flying</u> to an exotic destination.

1. Alana Smiley <u>is loving</u> to buy clothing. At this moment, she <u>is wear</u> designer
clothing. She <u>not care</u> about debts. Right now, she <u>buying</u> new boots that cost
$400. At this moment, she <u>is pay</u> for the boots with her credit card.

---

2. Alana <u>is knowing</u> that her credit card bill <u>is</u> really high. In fact, she <u>have</u> a

$10,000 debt. At this moment, Alana's debt <u>is grow</u> quickly. These days, she

<u>is not acting</u> responsibly. Every month, she <u>make</u> the minimum payment of

$42. So each month, she <u>is pays</u> only a few cents on her debt, and the rest

of the payment <u>goes</u> toward the monthly interest and fees.

UNIT Review

Answer the following questions. If you don't know an answer, go back and review the appropriate section.

1. What are some key words that mean "right now"? Write three words or phrases.

   _____

2. Write the correct form of the verb "speak" in the spaces below. Then explain why you chose that verb form.

   a) Christina _____ Greek.

   Reason: _____

   b) Christina _____ Greek with her friend right now.

   Reason: _____

3. Underline and correct the verb errors in the sentences below. Then explain why the sentences are incorrect.

   a) Every day, Christina is driving to work alone.   _____

   Reason: _____

   b) Right now, she not taking the train.   _____

   Reason: _____

   c) At this moment, she is text her best friend.   _____

   Reason: _____

4. Write the contracted negative form of each verb. Then write the question form.

	CONTRACTED NEGATIVE FORM	QUESTION FORM
EXAMPLE: He is talking.	<u>isn't talking</u>	<u>Is he talking?</u>
a) She is chatting.	_____	_____
b) They are typing.	_____	_____
c) He needs money.	_____	_____

Final Review

PART A

Fill in the blanks with a simple present or present progressive verb.

EXAMPLE: Oscar Romero (work, not) _doesn't work_ during the summer months.

1. At this moment, my friend Oscar (sit) _____ on his bike. Oscar (love) _____ to cycle.

2. Oscar is a cyclist. He frequently (visit) _____ this nature trail because a beautiful forest surrounds it.

3. Oscar (want) _____ to participate in the Tour de France one day. Right now, he (practise) _____.

4. At this moment, I (ride, not) _____ my bike. I (relax) _____ in the sun.

5. It is quite beautiful. At this moment, some people (eat) _____ at a picnic table, and some children (play) _____. Every morning, people (come) _____ to this park to do many things.

PART B

Write appropriate questions in the spaces provided. The answers to the questions are in bold.

6. Mr. Forzani sells **bicycles**.

   _____

7. That bike costs **about $1000**.

   _____

8. Oscar is riding his bike **because he is preparing for a race**.

   _____

9. The bike race is **at 2 p.m.**

   _____

10. Oscar has a lot of trophies **because he is a great cyclist**.

   _____

WRITING

A PUBLIC PLACE

Write eight sentences describing what is happening in the picture. Then write five questions. Use –*ing* verbs because the action is happening now.

Sentences

1. _____
2. _____
3. _____
4. _____
5. _____
6. _____
7. _____
8. _____

Questions

1. _____
2. _____
3. _____
4. _____
5. _____

Simple Past

Preview

WHAT IS THE SIMPLE PAST?

The **simple past** indicates that an action was completed at a definite time in the past. There are regular and irregular past tense verbs.

Regular	*Last year, the sports area **opened**.*
Irregular	*Yesterday, Eric **lost** his hockey stick.*

IRREGULAR VERB PUZZLE

First, determine the simple past form of the verbs. Then highlight them in the puzzle. The verbs could be written in any direction (up, down, sideways, or diagonally).

- buy _____
- cut _____
- do _____
- drink _____
- eat _____

- have _____
- give _____
- go ___went___
- feel _____
- know _____

- keep _____
- make _____
- meet _____
- put _____
- ride _____

- say _____
- sit _____
- teach _____
- take _____

W	S	T	A	U	G	H	T
E	R	O	D	E	S	A	T
N	B	O	U	G	H	T	M
T	H	K	N	E	W	E	A
U	G	D	E	C	D	I	D
S	A	I	D	P	U	T	E
H	V	F	E	L	T	T	T
M	E	T	D	R	A	N	K

After you finish finding the verbs, put the remaining letters in the spaces below to form a word that means "close" as in "Close the door, please."

____ ____ ____ ____ ____

© PEARSON LONGMAN • REPRODUCTION PROHIBITED

Reading and Listening

IDENTIFY SIMPLE PAST VERBS

Fill in the blanks with verbs in the simple past form. Choose from the verbs below. On the Companion Website, listen to an audio recording of the reading. You can correct your answers.

be	fight	kick	run	throw
do	have	play	swim	try

1. Sports are as old as humans. The first sports

_____ probably hunting games.

2. In ancient Greece, people _____

running competitions. **3.** The person who

_____ the fastest received honours.

4. In one competition, athletes _____

a heavy disk for a great distance. **5.** In 4000 BC,

in China, people _____ gymnastics.

6. Also, around 200 BC, the Chinese _____ a team sport called Cuju.

7. Using their feet, players _____ a ball through a small hole in a piece

of silk. The silk hung from two high poles. **8.** Ancient Greek paintings show water

sports. People _____ across lakes in races. **9.** Also, in many past

societies, people _____ contact sports. **10.** On elevated platforms,

wrestlers _____ each other.

Simple Past: Forms and Usage

Use the **simple past** when an action was completed at a definite time in the past.
Last Friday, we **went** to a concert.

Last Friday,	Saturday	Sunday	Monday	Today
5th	**6th**	**7th**	**8th**	**9th**

we **went** to
a concert.

Key Words: ago, five years ago, in 2006, last week, when I was a child, yesterday

AFFIRMATIVE, QUESTION, AND NEGATIVE FORMS

Review the forms of the simple past.

All Verbs Except *Be*

AFFIRMATIVE FORM	QUESTION FORM (Add *did*.)	NEGATIVE FORM (Add *did not*.)
I He She It } **slept**. You We They	**Did** I he she it } **sleep**? you we they	I He She It } **did not sleep**. You (didn't) We They

Be

AFFIRMATIVE FORM	QUESTION FORM (Move position of *be*.)	NEGATIVE FORM (Add *not*.)
I He She **was** late. It	**Was** I he she late? it	I He She **was not** late. It (wasn't)
You We **were** late. They	**Were** you we late? they	You We **were not** late. They (weren't)

REGULAR SIMPLE PAST VERBS

There are both regular and irregular past tense verbs. Regular simple past verbs end in *–ed* and generally don't appear on verb lists (such as the one at the back of this book) because of their standard form. Review some spelling rules.

LAST LETTER(S) OF VERB	EXAMPLE	*–ED* FORM	RULE
silent *–e*	smile	smil**ed**	Just add *–d*.
consonant + *–y*	study	stud**ied**	Change the *–y* to *–i* and add *–ed*.
vowel + *–y*	stay	stay**ed**	Just add *–ed*.
consonant-vowel-consonant (in one syllable verbs)	shop	shop**ped**	Double the last letter. **Exception:** words that end in *–x* or *–w* (*fix* ▶ *fixed*).
consonant-vowel-consonant (in verbs of more than one syllable)	re**fer** o**mit**	refe**rred** omi**tted**	Double the last letter when the verb ends in a stressed syllable*.
	BUT		
	open **ha**ppen	open**ed** happen**ed**	If the verb doesn't end in a stressed syllable, just add *–ed*.

* To know which syllable is stressed, refer to your dictionary or visit an online dictionary. The stressed syllable is indicated with a heavy black mark (') or with bold font.

IRREGULAR SIMPLE PAST VERBS

Some simple past verbs do not end in any specific letter. For a list of irregular simple past verbs, see Appendix 1 on pages 138–139.

QUESTION WORDS

QUESTION WORD	REFERS TO	QUESTION WORD	REFERS TO
Who	**a person** · **Who** are you? **Who** do you work with?	How	**a method or degree** **How** did you make this? **How** cold is it?
What	**a thing** **What** is your name?	How long	**a period of time** **How long** is the movie?
When	**a time** **When** does the show start?	How far	**a distance** **How far** is Laval from here?
Where	**a place** **Where** do you live?	How often	**the frequency of an activity** **How often** do you see a dentist?
Why	**a reason** **Why** is he late?	How much / How many	**an amount of something** **How much** does it cost? **How many** people are there?
		How old	**age** **How old** is Jamilla?

Practice

EXERCISE 1 WAS AND WERE

PART A

Write *was* or *were* in the spaces provided.

> **EXAMPLE:** Ancient Aztecs <u>were</u> in Mexico.

1. Over 3000 years ago, a popular Aztec ball game _____ dangerous.

2. The rubber ball _____ very hard.

3. Spectators _____ in the stadium.

4. The players _____ under a lot of pressure.

5. The stone hoop _____ on a wall.

Stone hoop for ancient Aztec game

PART B

Make the verbs in the following sentences negative. Use the contracted negative form.

> **EXAMPLE:** The players were happy.   weren't

6. The losing team was safe.   _____

7. The hole in the stone hoop was very large.   _____

8. The players were lazy.   _____

9. The three brothers were good players.   _____

TIP

There Was and *There Were*

Note the difference between *there was* and *there were*.

There was one thing.   **There were** two or more things.

EXERCISE 2 *THERE WAS/THERE WERE*

Describe items from a crime scene. Write questions and answers. Use the correct form of *there + be* in each complete sentence.

EXAMPLE: Question: _Was there_ a blue pen?
Answer: _There was_ a blue pen.

1. Question: _____ any fingerprints?

   Answer: _____

2. Question: _____ a black gun?

   Answer: _____

3. Question: _____ any paper clips?

   Answer: _____

4. Question: _____ a red lighter?

   Answer: _____

5. Question: _____ a purple feather?

   Answer: _____

EXERCISE 3 QUESTION WORDS

Write appropriate question words in the spaces provided. If you need help, refer to the Question Words chart on page 38.

EXAMPLE: We went to **Paris**.   _where_____

1. I went to bed **at 11 p.m.**   _____

2. He left **because he was tired**.   _____

3. I talked to **Mr. Jones**.   _____

4. We ate **in a restaurant**.   _____

5. It's **a desk**.   _____

6. It costs **$300**.   _____

7. He fixed it **with a hammer**.   _____

8. I visit him **twice a year**.   _____

9. He is **seventeen years old**.   _____

10. The restaurant is **twelve kilometres** from here. _____

11. There are **one hundred people** in the room. _____

12. We went there **for three weeks**. _____

EXERCISE 4 SIMPLE PAST QUESTIONS (*BE*)

Change the following sentences into questions using the simple past form. The answer to each question is in bold.

> **EXAMPLE:** The Winter X Games were **in Aspen**.
> <u>Where were the Winter X Games?</u>

1. The first X Games were **in Vermont**.

   _____

2. It was **an extreme sports and music festival**.

   _____

3. **Yes**, the festival was popular.

   _____

4. The spectators were happy **because they enjoyed extreme sports**.

   _____

5. The tickets were **$125**.

   _____

6. The best skateboarder was **Tony Hawk**.

   _____

PRONUNCIATION HELP WITH ONLINE DICTIONARIES

Many dictionaries are available online. On some sites, such as *dictionary.reference.com*, the stressed syllable is indicated in bold, and by clicking on the loudspeaker, you can hear the pronunciation of the word.

de·vel·op   ◀)) [dih-**vel**-*uh*p]

From *dictionary.reference.com*

EXERCISE 5 SPELLING OF REGULAR SIMPLE PAST VERBS

Write the simple past form of each verb. (If necessary, refer to the spelling rules on page 37.)

> **EXAMPLE:** stop   <u>stopped</u>

1. carry   _____   4. marry   _____

2. stay   _____   5. share   _____

3. shop   _____   6. rain   _____

To hear the correct pronunciation of simple past verbs and to try additional exercises, visit the Companion Website.

7. fail	_____	12. study	_____
8. slap	_____	13. plan	_____
9. hope	_____	14. open	_____
10. wash	_____	15. prefer	_____
11. remain	_____	16. happen	_____

TIP

Irregular Verbs

Learn to spell the irregular verbs in Appendix 1.

EXERCISE 6 IRREGULAR PAST VERBS

Work with a partner to fill in the blanks. Use the simple past form of each verb. Be careful; some verbs may be irregular.

> **EXAMPLE:** In the 1940s, someone (invent) _invented_ a new sport.

1. In the 1940s, most children (ride) _____ bicycles. Then a new sport (begin) _____. The inventor (give) _____ the name "skateboard" to his invention. He (attach) _____ roller skate wheels to a board.

2. During the 1940s, some youths (buy) _____ skateboards. They (take) _____ risks, and they (have) _____ many accidents. Bicycles (be) _____ not as dangerous as skateboards.

3. In the late 1950s, an inventor (make) _____ improvements to the device that holds the wheels. Skateboards (become) _____ safer.

4. In 1961, in California, many surfers (begin) _____ skateboarding because the sport required similar skills to surfing. Some skaters (do) _____ a variety of tricks. During a three-year period, stores (sell) _____ about 50 million skateboards. Then, in 1965, the popularity of skateboarding (fall) _____ once again.

NEGATIVE FORMS

To form negative simple past verbs, place *did not* between the subject and the verb.

*Sheila did **not** sell many tickets.*	(contraction: ***didn't sell***)
*Those men did **not** watch the movie.*	(contraction: ***didn't watch***)

Exception: When the main verb is *be* (*was, were*), just add *not*.

*The story was **not** suspenseful.*	(contraction: ***wasn't***)
*They were **not** happy.*	(contraction: ***weren't***)

EXERCISE 7 AFFIRMATIVE AND NEGATIVE FORMS

Write the affirmative or negative form of the verb in parentheses. For negative verbs, use the contracted form.

> **EXAMPLE:** Edward (have, not) <u>didn't have</u> a skateboard.

1. In the 1960s, many parents (like, not) _____ the skateboarding trend. Too many children (have) _____ serious skateboarding accidents. According to Michael Brooke, author of *The Concrete Wave*, many accidents (happen) _____ because the clay wheels on the 1960s skateboards (grip, not) _____ the road very well. The sport (be, not) _____ popular again until the 1970s.

2. In 1972, Frank Nasworthy (make) _____ urethane wheels for skateboards. He (know, not) _____ if his idea would be popular. He (have, not) _____ a lot of money to promote his product. But soon, some surfers (discover) _____ his product. They (use, not) _____ boards with clay wheels again.

QUESTION FORMS

Add an auxiliary (*did*) before the subject and use the base form of the main verb.

Burke won many medals. **Did** Burke <u>win</u> many medals?

base form

Exception: *Be* doesn't need an auxiliary verb.

When the verb is a form of *be*, place *was* or *were* before the subject.

Sunglasses were popular in the past. **Were** they popular in the past?

EXERCISE 8 QUESTION AND NEGATIVE FORMS

Write the simple past form of the verbs in parentheses. Then write the contracted negative forms and the appropriate questions. The answers to the questions are in bold.

> **EXAMPLE:** Sarah Burke (learn) <u>learned</u> **to ski.**
> Question: <u>What did Sarah Burke learn?</u>   <u>didn't learn</u>

1. Sarah Burke (become) _____ famous **by competing in skiing competitions**.   _____

   Question: _____

2. She (live) _____ in Ontario **for nineteen years**. _____

   Question: _____

3. She (win) _____ **three** gold medals. _____

   Question: _____

4. ESPN (call) _____ Burke **the world's best
   female skier**. _____

   Question: _____

5. Sports fans (be) _____ happy **because women
   competed in the X Games**. _____

   Question: _____

6. Burke (be) _____ in **three** movies. _____

   Question: _____

7. She (appear) _____ in skiing films **because
   she earned a lot of money**. _____

   Question: _____

8. She (move) _____ to **Whistler, BC**. _____

   Question: _____

TIP

Use the Base Form of the Verb after *Did* and *To*

In the simple past, use the base form of verbs that follow *did* and *to*.

like	*change*
Leanne didn't ~~liked~~ her name.	She wanted to ~~changed~~ her name.

EXERCISE 9 IDENTIFY ERRORS

Underline the errors involving the simple past. Then correct
the errors in the spaces provided.

EXAMPLE:
He didn't <u>wanted</u> a quiet life.   <u>want</u>

1. Jaime Bravo is born in
   Mexico City. _____

2. Bravo did'nt have an easy
   childhood. _____

3. He not stayed in the ghetto. _____

4. He wanted to learned about
   bullfighting. _____

5. He becomed a bullfighter
   when he was twenty-six. _____

6 During his life, Bravo did not tried ordinary jobs. _____

7. Did Bravo was a great bullfighter? _____

8. He maked some movies about bullfighting. _____

9. Why he risked his life? _____

10. Bravo haved relationships with Hollywood actresses. _____

11. He liked to drove very fast, and in 1970 he died
in a car accident. _____

12. In the past, many people was happy to see bullfights. _____

↻ UNIT Review

Answer the following questions. If you don't know an answer, go back and review the appropriate section.

1. Underline the key words used with the simple past.
last week   next Friday   now   sometimes   two days ago   yesterday

2. Correct the verb errors in the sentences below. Then explain why the sentences are incorrect.

a) Why did the artist painted portraits? _____

Reason: _____

b) There was three people at the show. _____

Reason: _____

c) He wanted to captured the person's spirit. _____

Reason: _____

d) He stoped the car and took a picture. _____

Reason: _____

3. Write the contracted negative form of the verb. Then write the yes/no question form.

a) He was alone. _____

Question: _____

b) They were late. _____

Question: _____

c) He liked the show. _____

Question: _____

PART A

Write the simple past form of the verb in the space provided.

EXAMPLE: In 2002, Mark Zuckerberg (have, not) <u>didn't have</u> a lot of money.

1. In 2003, Mark Zuckerberg (write) _____ a computer program called Facemash.

2. At that time, the website (be, not) _____ open to the public.

3. In 2003, most Harvard students (be, not) _____ aware of the site.

4. Some friends helped Zuckerberg. He (work, not) _____ alone.

5. When he created his site, Zuckerberg (follow, not) _____ the rules.

6. He (take) _____ photos from protected parts of Harvard's computer network.

7. In 2004, Zuckerberg (have)

   _____ some problems.

8. He (choose) _____ a new name for his website: Facebook.

9. In 2005, many people (make)

   _____ Facebook pages.

10. Zuckerberg (become) _____ a very rich man.

PART B

Underline the error in the sentence, and write the correction in the space provided. Write *C* if the sentence has no errors.

EXAMPLE: In 2004, Zuckerberg <u>haved</u> a great idea.   had

11. In 2007, he decided to talked with Microsoft investors. _____

12. He didn't planned to sell part of his company. _____

13. Zuckerberg, Eduardo Saverin, and three other friends was happy with the investment deal. _____

14. They didn't expect to become instant millionaires. _____

15. In 2011, do Zuckerberg spend a lot of his money? _____

PART C

Write questions for the following sentences. The clues to the questions are in bold.

> **EXAMPLE:** Facebook became popular **in 2005**.
> <u>When did Facebook become popular?</u>

16. Zuckerberg had a party **because his social networking site was popular**.

   _____

17. **Yes**, he earned a lot of money.

   _____

18. He became a billionaire **in 2007**.

   _____

19. He bought a house **in Ireland**.

   _____

20. Some students were jealous **because they didn't own part of the company**.

   _____

WRITING

Write a paragraph about a movie or television show that you saw recently. Describe what happened in the show. Then underline the simple past verbs.

   _____

   _____

   _____

   _____

   _____

   _____

   _____

   _____

   _____

   _____

   _____

   _____

   _____

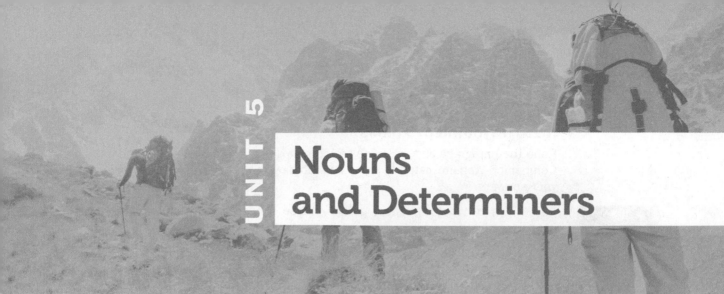

Nouns and Determiners

Preview

WHAT IS A NOUN?

A **noun** is a person, place, or thing. A **count noun** can be counted and has a plural form. A **noncount noun** cannot be counted and has only a singular form. Often, noncount nouns refer to categories of objects or abstract concepts.

noncount noun	count noun
*We had a lot of **homework**.*	*We have three **assignments**.*

CATEGORIES COMPETITION

Work with a partner. Describe what you see in the pictures. First, decide what the category is. (The category is a noncount noun.) Then list the items. Put *a*, *an*, or a number before each item.

Category: jewellery

Items: a ring

_____

_____

_____

_____

_____

Category: _____

Items: _____

_____

_____

_____

_____

_____

Category: _____

Items: _____

_____

_____

_____

_____

_____

Reading and Listening

IDENTIFY CORRECT FORMS

Read the paragraph and underline the correct word in parentheses. On the Companion Website, listen to an audio recording of the reading. You can correct your answers.

1. What is happening (this / those / these) days? **2.** Many people are putting private (information / informations) online. **3.** In fact, (beliefs / believes) about privacy are changing daily. **4.** One of the most popular (website / websites) is YouTube. **5.** Some (childs / children / childrens) put personal videos online. **6.** For example, ten-(year / years)-old Camilla has a YouTube page that she updates weekly. **7.** She talks about her (homework / homeworks) and her friends. **8.** Viewers enter the child's bedroom, where they see her (furniture / furnitures) and her clothing. **9.** She wants to put every (activity / activities) online. **10.** Too (much / many) people put private information online.

Nouns and Determiners: Forms and Usage

Nouns are words that refer to people, places, or things. Most nouns have singular and plural forms.

SPELLING: PLURAL NOUNS

	SINGULAR	PLURAL
Most plural nouns simply end in –s.	girl house	girl**s** house**s**
Add –es to nouns ending in –s, –ch, –sh, –x, z, or –o.	kiss match box	kiss**es** match**es** box**es**
When nouns end in –f or –fe, change the –f or –fe to –v and add –es.	shelf knife	shel**ves** kni**ves**
When nouns end in a consonant + –y, change –y to –ies.	factory lady	factor**ies** lad**ies**
When nouns end in vowel + –y, just add –s.	boy	boy**s**

IRREGULAR PLURALS

Some nouns have irregular plural forms. These irregular forms do not need an additional –s.

child	▶	**children**		mouse	▶	**mice**
man	▶	**men**		foot	▶	**feet**
woman	▶	**women**		tooth	▶	**teeth**
person	▶	**people**		fish	▶	**fish**

PLURAL NOUNS WITH A SINGULAR MEANING

Some nouns always have a plural form but a singular meaning.

economics   mathematics   mechanics
news   politics   physics

*My brother studied **physics**.   Now he is taking a course in **mechanics**.*

COUNT AND NONCOUNT NOUNS

Count nouns refer to people, places, or things that you can count, such as *girl* or *toy*. Count nouns have both a singular and a plural form.

*I have a **dog**.   My brother has two **dogs**.*

Noncount nouns cannot be counted. They have only a singular form.

*We have too much **homework**.   We must do a lot of **research**.*

To express the quantity of a noncount noun, we use expressions that describe amounts such as *types of*, *a lot of*, or *pieces of*.

*I received three <u>pieces of</u> **mail**.   We need <u>a lot of</u> **information**.*

COMMON NONCOUNT NOUNS

CATEGORIES OF OBJECTS			FOOD		ABSTRACT NOUNS		
clothing	jewellery	money	bread	meat	advice	health	research
equipment	luggage	music	cheese	milk	evidence	knowledge	time (free time)
furniture	machinery	software	fruit	wine	experience	luck	trouble
homework	mail	work			information	proof	violence

DETERMINERS

Using *Much*, *Many*, and *A Lot of*

TERM	USE WITH	EXAMPLE
much	noncount nouns	I have too **much** work these days.
many	count nouns	Does London have **many** museums?
a lot of	both count and noncount nouns	You have **a lot of** friends. Do you have **a lot of** money?

This, *That*, *These*, *Those*

TERM	USAGE	EXAMPLE
this (singular) **these** (plural)	refers to things that are near the speaker in time or place	**This** burger is good. **These** fries are also tasty. **These** days, it is sunny.
that (singular) **those** (plural)	refers to things that are far from the speaker in time or place	Do you see **those** photos in **that** window? In 2004, there were severe snowstorms. **That** was a very cold year.

Articles

TERM	USAGE	EXAMPLE
a, an	refers to a general person, place, or thing	Myles needs **a** new shirt. He wants **an** apple.
the	refers to one or more specific nouns	**The** shirts in that store are expensive.

Practice

EXERCISE 1 PLURAL NOUNS

Fill in the blanks with one of the following nouns. Use the plural form of each noun.

baby   example   leaf   person
child   foot   man   woman

1. Some _____, both male and female, are amazing photographers.
   Everyone knows famous _____ such as Man Ray, Yousuf Karsh,
   and Ansel Adams. In recent years, _____ have also become
   successful. _____ include Cindy Sherman, Moyra Davie, and
   Annie Leibowitz.

2. Last week, I bought a great book of photos by Anne Geddes. She takes photos
   of infants and _____ who are two to four years old. Often, she
   places tiny ten-month-old _____ in large green _____.
   They look like little flowers. Their tiny hands and _____ are so cute.

EXERCISE 2 IDENTIFY PLURAL ERRORS

Correct fifteen errors in the underlined plural nouns. Write *C* above the plural nouns
that are correct.

                             companies
EXAMPLE: Many <u>companys</u> break the law.

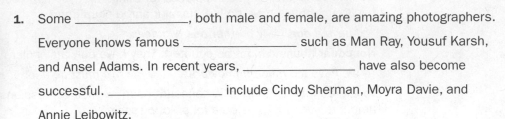

1. I am interested in <u>politic</u>. I watch the <u>news</u> on television every night.

2. In many <u>countrys</u>, <u>childs</u> have difficult <u>lifes</u>.

3. In Vietnam, some <u>familys</u> need their <u>sons</u> and <u>daughter</u> to work.

4. For example, the garment industry may force very young <u>womens</u>
   to sew for many <u>hours</u>.

5. For seven <u>days</u> a week, many <u>ladys</u> make <u>toys</u>.

6. Sometimes small <u>boyes</u> and <u>girls</u> work in <u>factorys</u>.

7. Those <u>childrens</u> put sharp <u>knifes</u> in <u>boxes</u>.

8. They stand on their <u>feets</u> all day.

9. <u>Persons</u> who study <u>economic</u> should learn about child labour.

EXERCISE 3 IDENTIFY NONCOUNT NOUNS

Write the plural form beside the nouns that can be counted. Write *NC* next to the noncount nouns.

EXAMPLE: dog <u>dogs</u>   advice   <u>NC</u>

1. work _____
2. person _____
3. music _____
4. song _____
5. dollar _____
6. money _____
7. child _____

8. shirt _____
9. clothing _____
10. information _____
11. suitcase _____
12. luggage _____
13. essay _____
14. homework _____

For extra practice with nouns and determiners, visit the Companion Website.

SPECIAL RULES

One of the ...

Use a plural noun after the expression *one of the*.

   <u>One of the</u> most difficult **jobs** is nursing.

Each/Every

Use a singular noun after *each* and *every*.

   <u>Each</u> **day**, the boss speaks to <u>every</u> **employee**.

Adjectives are never plural.

An adjective describes a noun or pronoun. Never put an *–s* or *–es* on an adjective.

   other
   I have ~~others~~ **priorities**.

   great
   These are ~~greats~~ **deals**.

EXERCISE 4 SINGULAR AND PLURAL NOUNS

Change the italicized words to the plural form, if necessary. If you cannot use the plural form, write *X* in the blank. Remember that adjectives are never plural.

EXAMPLE: Bill has two job<u>s</u>. He earns a lot of money <u>X</u>.

1. Aline Tugend is a journalist for *The New York Times*. In one of her *great*____
   *article*____, Tugend discusses stressed business *traveller*____. According
   to Tugend, frequent work-related travel, which is defined as six or more
   business *trip*____ each *year*____, can cause eating, sleeping, and breathing
   *disorder*____. There is a lot of *research*____ on the subject. Sleep and stress
   are *important*____ *topic*____.

2. Antonio Morales travels to many *different*____ *place*____. He spends a lot of *time*____ on *airplane*____ and in many hotel *room*____. He eats in *different*____ *restaurant*____ every *night*____. He has a lot of *problem*____ communicating with his two *young*____ *daughter*____ because he rarely sees them. One of his *daughter*____ is performing in a school play, but Morales will miss the show. She does not give her father a lot of *information*____ about her life.

MUCH OR MANY

Use *many* with count nouns. You can use *many* with affirmative, negative, and question forms.

> *Does London have **many** <u>museums</u>?*   *There are **many** interesting <u>attractions</u>.*

Use *much* with noncount nouns. Use *much* in question and negative forms. In affirmative forms, use *a lot* instead of *much* unless you refer to an excessive amount of something, such as *too much* or *so much*.

> *How **much** <u>money</u> do you have?*   *Ben doesn't have **much** <u>work</u>.*
> *He has too **much** <u>free time</u> these days.*

Use *a lot* with count and noncount nouns.

> *Kara has **a lot** of <u>free time</u>.*   *She also has **a lot** of <u>friends</u>.*

TIP

Money

When you enquire about a price, ask "***How much** is it?*" Use *much*, because the word *money* is implied.

> ***How much** (money) is the train ticket?*

EXERCISE 5 *MUCH AND MANY*

Write *much* or *many* in the blanks.

1. Tourism is an important industry in _____ countries. When a disaster strikes, there is not _____ work for the local people. For example, after the Asian tsunami, _____ people lost their lives, and others lost their jobs.

2. I am visiting Greece. I did not receive _____ information about Athens. There are probably _____ museums. Right now, _____ men and women are visiting the Acropolis. How _____ does it cost to view the ruins? We do not have _____ free time, so maybe we can visit the ruins later.

THIS, THAT, THESE, THOSE

This and **these** refer to people and things that are physically close to the speaker in time or place.

That and **those** refer to people and things that are physically distant from the speaker in time or place.

Near the speaker
This (singular)
These (plural)

Far from the speaker
That (singular)
Those (plural)

Singular	**This** is my house.	**That** is my sister's car.
Plural	**These** shoes are dirty.	**Those** cars are going too fast.

EXERCISE 6 *THIS, THAT, THESE, THOSE*

Write *this, that, these,* or *those* in the blanks.

EXAMPLE: What are __these__ marks on my shirt?

1. I am standing near a window. Come and look out _____ window. What is _____ strange object in the sky? It is flying.

2. Look at _____ hot-air balloons in the sky. Do you see _____ people in the distance? They are waving at us.

3. In the early 1990s, some people started the hot-air balloon festival. _____ were exciting years. I was born in 1991. The festival began in _____ year.

4. There are some binoculars beside me. I will use _____ binoculars to get a better look. Also, right beside me there is a telescope. _____ telescope is also very useful.

5. _____ hot-air balloons are so beautiful! I love to watch the sky _____ days.

EXERCISE 7 IDENTIFY ERRORS

Correct ten errors in the underlined words below. If the word is correct, write *C* above it.

              These   C
EXAMPLE: <u>This</u> shoes are tight. I really like <u>those</u> shoes that you are wearing.

1. I don't like <u>this</u> newspapers that are on the table. They are boring. <u>This</u> magazine, however, is interesting. There are <u>much</u> good articles. A magazine subscription does not cost <u>much</u> money.

2. Look out the window at <u>these</u> people across the street. Why are <u>that</u> people angry? Why is <u>this</u> girl in the red shirt yelling? Perhaps <u>those</u> students are protesting. They have <u>much</u> complaints. Wow, now <u>many</u> reporters are watching the action. They are taking <u>much</u> photos of the crowd.

3. My grandmother was born during the 1940s. <u>These</u> were difficult years. Women did not have <u>much</u> rights. I have a photograph of my grandmother from <u>this</u> time. In the photo, she was very young and beautiful.

A AND *AN*

A and *an* are indefinite (general) articles. They mean "one." Place *a* or *an* before a singular noun.

Use *a* before words that begin with a consonant: **a** friend, **a** house.

Exception: When *u* sounds like *you*, put *a* before it: **a** union, **a** university.

Use *an* before words that begin with a vowel: **an** apple, **an** umbrella.

Exception: Use *an* before words that begin with silent *h:* **an** hour, **an** honest man.

EXERCISE 8 *A* OR *AN*

Put *a, an,* or *X* (meaning nothing) in the spaces provided. You cannot put *a* or *an* before a plural count noun or a noncount noun.

EXAMPLE: Those are <u>X</u> great bikes.

1. My brother is _____ actor and I am _____ drummer.

2. My parents didn't expect to have _____ artist in the family, but now they have two.

3. I live in _____ nice apartment. My brother doesn't live in _____ apartment.

4. My brother owns _____ condo. He paid for it with _____ role on _____ TV soap opera. He played _____ hospital worker.

5. My brother creates _____ interesting characters. He earns _____ good salary.

6. He has _____ several film roles. He usually plays _____ honest and friendly man. Each character is _____ happy person.

7. My parents wanted me to be _____ accountant, so I went to _____ university in Ontario.

8. However, I dropped out after _____ semester, and now I am _____ artist.

THE

Use **the** to indicate a specific noun (or specific nouns). *The* can be placed before both singular and plural nouns.

        general   specific
*I need to find **a** new shirt. **The** shirts in that store are expensive.*

Common Errors with *The*

Do not put *the* before the following:

- sports   ▶ He plays soccer.
- languages   ▶ She speaks Mandarin.
- most city, province, state, or country names ▶ Juan lives in Mexico.
  (Some exceptions are the United States and
  the Netherlands.)
- nature (meaning outdoors in the wilderness) ▶ I love to walk in nature.

EXERCISE 9   *A, AN, OR THE*

Put *a, an, the,* or *X* (meaning nothing) in the spaces provided.

    EXAMPLE: I think that <u>X</u> life is sometimes difficult.
          <u>The</u> life of a fast-food employee can be particularly rough.

1. Vladimir is _____ employee at _____ fast-food restaurant. He has to be at _____ restaurant every morning at 8:30 a.m. He drives _____ old Honda Civic to work. Vladimir is also _____ student. He wants to receive _____ university degree in education.

2. Vladimir left Russia six years ago. He can speak _____ English and _____ French, but he prefers to speak _____ Russian. Vladimir usually speaks _____ French with the customers. After work, he walks in _____ woods near his home because he loves _____ nature.

3. At university, Vladimir is studying _____ education because he loves _____ children. Did you see _____ photo of his son in his wallet? His son loves sports and plays _____ hockey and _____ soccer. Vladimir wants to be _____ teacher, but he is also interested in _____ history and _____ philosophy.

EXERCISE 10 IDENTIFY ERRORS

The following sentences include errors with *a, an,* and *the*. Also look for errors with *all day* and *every day*. Correct fifteen errors.

 an
EXAMPLE: The director is ˄unusual person.

1. Sean Penn directs a great movies.

2. I have big poster of the movie *Into the Wild*.

3. The movie is about a man who loved the nature.

4. I love the nature too. Yesterday, I spent all the day outdoors.

5. Last week, it rained all days for a couple of hours. From Monday to Friday, it rained.

6. In the future, I will be an director, or maybe I will be writer.

7. I would love to write a great sports movies about the basketball and the soccer.

8. I don't have an other plan for my future.

9. These days, there are alot of movies online, so people download them.

10. I will make movies in the English and the French because I am bilingual.

⟳ UNIT Review

Answer the following questions. If you don't know an answer, go back and review the appropriate section.

1. Can *a* or *an* be placed before a plural noun? _____
   Explain why: _____

2. What are the plural forms of the following nouns?
   a) person _____
   b) boy _____
   c) hobby _____
   d) match _____
   e) man _____
   f) child _____

3. Write *C* next to the count nouns and *NC* next to the noncount nouns.
   a) women _____   d) dollar _____
   b) work _____   e) equipment _____
   c) money _____   f) tire _____

4. Correct the errors in the following sentences.

   a) One of my favourite movie is *Avatar*, and I will probably watch it

      an other time.

   b) I watch alot of movies every weekends.

   c) I go to movies alone or with others peoples.

   d) That cars are driving too fast.

   e) This days, I feel very tired.

   f) I want to have much children in the future.

COMPANION web+ Need more practice? Visit the Companion Website and try additional exercises.

Final Review

Underline the appropriate words in parentheses below. Note that X means no word is needed.

1. Every (country / countrys / countries) has special (holiday / holidays) and celebrations. (Persons / Peoples / People) do special things on (that / those) days. (Much / Many) places have (different / differents) customs.

2. In (the / X) Japan, there is (a / an / the / X) unusual custom every February 14th. On Valentine's Day, (woman / women / womens) must buy chocolate for their husbands and male colleagues. (Childs / Childrens / Children) don't receive chocolate.

3. During (a / the / X) month of February, department stores advertise (much / many) products. For example, a department store near (the / a / X) Sony Building in downtown Tokyo sells two (type / types) of chocolates. *Giri* chocolate is for (a / an / X) male friends and family members, and *honmei* chocolate is for husbands and boyfriends. The stores don't provide (much / many) (information / informations) about the dangers of eating too (much / many) sugar. February 14th is one of the busiest (day / days) of the year for chocolate stores.

4. Kaori Kato is (a / an / X) Japanese student, and she is also (a / an / X) accountant. She speaks (the / X) English, and she loves to play (the / X) soccer. Last February 14th, she bought her boyfriend (the / a / an) box of chocolates, and on (this / that) day, they celebrated together. (This / These) year, she wants to do something special. She will make candy at home. On February 13th, she will cook all (day / days).

5. One month after Valentine's Day, there is (an other / another) holiday. White Day is on March 14th, and it is for (a / an / X) females. They get (alot / a lot) of gifts on White Day.

 **WRITING**   On a separate piece of paper, write a paragraph about your possessions. List some items that are in your bedroom. Which items are most valuable to you? Which items are useless?

UNIT 6

Future

Preview

WHAT IS THE FUTURE TENSE?

The **future** tense indicates that an action will occur at a future time. You can use *will* or *be going to* plus the verb.

In ten years, I **will have** *my own business. I'***m going to live** *in a big city.*

YOUR FUTURE HOUSE

A fortune teller predicts that you will buy your ideal house in ten years. What features will your house have? Work with a partner and create six sentences about your ideal house. Use *will* or *be going to* in your sentences.

EXAMPLE: The house will have a porch on the front.

_____

_____

_____

_____

_____

_____

_____

_____

_____

_____

_____

_____

Reading and Listening

IDENTIFY FUTURE TENSE VERBS

Fill in the blanks with appropriate future tense verbs. Choose from the list of verbs below. Use affirmative and negative forms. On the Companion Website, listen to an audio recording of the reading. You can correct your answers.

be	exist	grow	need	see
continue	find	look	react	watch

1. In the future, televisions probably _____ anymore.

2. Instead, humans _____ entertainment programs on wall-sized computers. 3. The screen _____ like a window.

4. The computer _____ to spoken commands. 5. People _____ remote controls anymore.

6. Perhaps, in 2050, the most powerful country in the world _____ China. 7. It _____ to have the world's largest population.

8. Many predict that China's economy _____ rapidly. 9. In the field of science, maybe someone _____ a cure for cancer.

10. I hope that I _____ some of those new discoveries.

Future: Forms and Usage

The future tense indicates that an action will occur at a future time. You can use *will* or *be going to* plus the verb.

Next April, I **will graduate**. My brother **is going to graduate** too.

Today	January	February	March	Next April

I **will graduate**.
He **is going to graduate**.

Key Words: soon, later, tomorrow, the day after tomorrow, next week, next month, one day, in five years

WILL AND (BE) GOING TO

Both *will* and *(be) going to* indicate a future action. You can use either form most of the time, but there are some small differences in meaning.

FUNCTION	FORM	EXAMPLE
Predictions	will/be going to	We **will graduate** next summer. We **are going to graduate** next summer.
Spontaneous actions	will	The phone is ringing. I **will answer** it.
Planned actions	be going to	I'm **going to sell** my old television.

AFFIRMATIVE, QUESTION, AND NEGATIVE FORMS

Will

AFFIRMATIVE FORM	QUESTION FORM (Move *will* before the subject.)	NEGATIVE FORM (Add *not*.)
I She He It You We They } **will study.**	**Will** I she he it you we they } **study?**	I She He It You We They } **will not study.** (won't)

Be going to

AFFIRMATIVE FORM		QUESTION FORM (Move *be* before the subject.)			NEGATIVE FORM (Add *not*.)	
I	**am going to eat.**	**Am**	I	**going to eat?**	I	**am not going to eat.**
She He It	**is going to eat.**	**Is**	she he it	**going to eat?**	She He It	**is not going to eat.** (isn't)
You We They	**are going to eat.**	**Are**	you we they	**going to eat?**	You We They	**are not going to eat.** (aren't)

Practice

EXERCISE 1 PREDICT THE FUTURE

PART A: *WILL*

Fill in the blanks with the correct form of *will*.

    EXAMPLE: Myriam (buy) <u>will buy</u> a car.

1. In the future, I (have) _____ a great life.

2. My children (love) _____ me.

3. My father (live) _____ for many years.

4. My sister (find) _____ a job easily.

5. We (build) _____ a new house.

To hear the correct pronunciation of the future tense and to try additional exercises, visit the Companion Website.

PART B: *BE GOING TO*

Fill in the blanks with *be going to* and the base form of the verb.

> **EXAMPLE:** Solar energy (become) <u>is going to become</u> popular.

6. Next fall (be) _____ beautiful.

7. The leaves (turn) _____ red and yellow.

8. We (drive) _____ across the country.

9. I (have) _____ a great time.

10. My daughter (write) _____ about the trip.

TIP

Will or *Be Going To*?

Use both *will* and *be going to* when you predict the future. For previously planned actions, use *be going to*. For spontaneous actions, use *will*.

Prediction   I **will pass**. You **are going to pass**, too.
Planned   I paid for my ticket. I **am going to fly** to Mexico next month.
Spontaneous The doorbell is ringing. I **will answer** it.

EXERCISE 2 *WILL* AND *BE GOING TO*

Read each sentence and explain why the underlined verb is *will* or *be going to*. Choose one of the following reasons: PL for a planned action; SP for a spontaneous action.

> **EXAMPLES:** I bought the tickets. I <u>am going to watch</u> the show soon. <u>PL</u>
>
>   The dishes are dirty. I <u>will wash</u> them. <u>SP</u>

1. The doorbell is ringing. I <u>will get</u> it. _____

2. I'<u>m going to save</u> some money and travel to Mexico. _____

3. My brother <u>is going to move</u> to Winnipeg. _____

4. I'<u>ll shovel</u> the snow. You don't have to do it. _____

5. We'<u>re going to have</u> a baby. It is due in three months. _____

NEGATIVE FORMS

To make future verbs negative, just add *not*.

> She **will <u>not</u> leave**.   (contraction: **won't**)
> He **is <u>not</u> going to eat**.   (contraction: **isn't**)
> They **are not going to run**.   (contraction: **aren't**)

PART A

Write the contracted negative form of the underlined verbs.

    EXAMPLE: In the future, scientists <u>will find</u> alien life forms.   <u>won't find</u>

1. The aliens <u>will resemble</u> humans.   _____
2. They <u>will have</u> ten fingers and toes.   _____
3. Some people <u>will meet</u> the aliens.   _____
4. They <u>are going to stay</u> on Earth.   _____
5. The aliens <u>will be</u> aggressive.   _____
6. It <u>is going to be</u> peaceful.   _____
7. You <u>are going to see</u> the aliens.   _____
8. The event <u>will happen</u> in my lifetime.   _____

QUESTION FORMS

Will

In question forms, move *will* before the subject.

  You will finish soon.   ***Will** you finish soon?*

Be Going To

In question forms, move *be* before the subject.

  They are going to finish soon.   ***Are** they going to finish soon?*

EXERCISE 4 WRITE QUESTIONS

Write questions for the following sentences. The answers are in bold.

    EXAMPLE: The new hospital will open **next year**.   <u>When will open?</u>

1. The new hospital is going to be expensive **because the equipment is valuable**.

  _____

2. Dr. Roy will find **a cure for cancer**.

  _____

3. The machine will cost **millions of dollars**.

  _____

4. A cure will be ready **in ten years**.

  _____

5. Scientists will test the drug on **mice**.

  _____

6. Mr. Lee is going to donate money **because he wants to help**.

   _____

7. Kim will donate **$50.**

   _____

8. It will take **three years** to build the hospital.

   _____

TIME CLAUSES

In sentences that indicate the future, use the present tense in time clauses. A time clause begins with a time marker such as *when*. Never use the future tense after the following time markers.

after	before	until
as soon as	unless	when

time marker +
future tense   present tense

Dylan **will learn** to drive <u>when</u> he **is** sixteen.

time marker +
present tense   future tense

<u>As soon as</u> he **has** his licence, he **will buy** a car.

EXERCISE 5 TIME CLAUSES

Underline and correct the verb errors in the sentences below. Note that the time markers are in bold.

                          finish

EXAMPLE: I will leave **as soon as** I <u>will finish</u> my work.

1. **When** Lyle will find a job, he will be very happy.

2. He will move out **as soon as** he will graduate from college.

3. **After** Lyle will leave, his parents will turn his bedroom into an office.

4. I will drive Lyle **unless** you will want to.

5. **When** Lyle will have his own place, he will feel independent.

6. **Before** I will visit Lyle, I will call you.

SHORT ANSWERS

You can answer questions with short answers. Simply repeat the subject and the auxiliary. It isn't necessary to repeat the verb.

| *Will you help me?* | Yes, **I will**. | OR | No, **I won't**. |
| *Are they happy?* | Yes, **they are**. | OR | No, **they aren't**. |

EXERCISE 6 SHORT ANSWERS

Answer the following questions with short answers. The questions are in the present, past, and future tenses.

EXAMPLE: Will you buy a house?   Yes, I ____will____. No, I ____won't____.

1. Are you working right now?   Yes, I _____. No, I _____.
2. Are we going to have a pension? Yes, we _____. No, we _____.
3. Will he pay for university?   Yes, he _____. No, he _____.
4. Will you retire at sixty-five?   Yes, I _____. No, I _____.
5. Do you want a flying car?   Yes, I _____. No, I _____.
6. Does Ted believe in climate change? Yes, he _____. No, he _____.
7. Are they going to buy computers? Yes, they _____. No, they _____.
8. Did Ben graduate?   Yes, he _____. No, he _____.
9. Will the future be better for us? Yes, it _____. No, it _____.

USING PRESENT TENSES TO INDICATE THE FUTURE

The **present progressive** can refer to a previously planned event that will happen in the near future.

> We **are leaving** tonight. We **are taking** the train.

The **simple present** can refer to schedules and timetables.

> The bus **arrives** at 9 a.m. It **leaves** at 9:15 a.m.

TIP

Never Write *Gonna*

Although people say *gonna*, it isn't a proper word. Always write *going to*.

>   **going to**
> I am **gonna** finish this project.

EXERCISE 7 IDENTIFY ERRORS

Correct errors in the underlined verbs. Write *C* if the verb is correct.

>   are you going to do
> **EXAMPLE:** What <u>are you gonna do</u> about climate change?

1. David Suzuki is a renowned scientist. He often criticizes politicians who <u>wo'nt act</u>

   to solve the climate change crisis.

2. Suzuki <u>be going to talk</u> about government inactivity.

3. Unless we <u>will start</u> to act now, Canada <u>will have</u> serious flooding on both

   coasts.

4. Tomorrow, Suzuki <u>will speaks</u> to university students.

5. He <u>is gonna lecture</u> about the possible effects of climate change, including

   a global rise in sea levels.

6. Polar ice caps <u>are going to melt</u>.

7. Many people <u>is going to</u> attend the lecture.

8. Why <u>Suzuki visiting</u> the university?

9. <u>Is he is going to change</u> people's attitudes?

10. <u>Do he will convince</u> young people to take action now?

11. The lecture <u>will lasts</u> for two hours.

12. He <u>will answering</u> questions after his lecture.

EXERCISE 8 PAST, PRESENT, AND FUTURE

Write the correct past, present, or future tense verb in the spaces provided.

> **EXAMPLE:** In the 1973, an inventor (create) <u>created</u> the first cellphone.

1. In the 1980s, most people (have, not) _____ a cellphone.

   There (be, not) _____ many people who needed one, and

   the models (be) _____ large and heavy. The first cellphone

   weighed nearly two kilograms. How much money (a cellphone, cost)

   _____ in 1984?

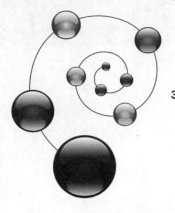

2. Today, some families (own) _____ three or more cellphones. My brother (have) _____ a cellphone, but he (use, not) _____ it very much. Why (everyone, need) _____ _____ a cellphone now?

3. In 2050, what (a cellphone, do) _____? How many functions (it, have) _____? What size (future phones, be) _____? Already, Nokia is working on a new phone. It (look, probably) _____ like a beaded necklace, and a bead (light) _____ up during a call.

↻ UNIT Review

Answer the following questions. If you don't know an answer, go back and review the appropriate section.

1. What is the negative form of *will*? _____

2. Underline and correct the verb errors in the sentences below. Then explain why the sentences are incorrect.

a) In the future, Brigitte is gonna visit China. _____

Reason: _____

b) She will flying with Air Canada. _____

Reason: _____

c) When I will have enough money, I will buy a car. _____

Reason: _____

3. Write the question and negative forms of the following sentences.

a) Jay will leave soon.

Question: _____

Negative: _____

b) They are going to buy a solar car.

Question: _____

Negative: _____

c) He is going to move.

Question: _____

Negative: _____

Final Review

PART A

Circle the letter of the correct answer.

1. According to the fortune teller, Samuel … a beautiful woman.

    a) will meeting   b) is going to meet   c) is gonna meet

2. She … in the same city as Samuel.

    a) won't are   b) will not to be   c) won't be

3. They … on an airplane.

    a) will meets   b) are gonna meet   c) will meet

4. What … to each other?

    a) are they going to say   b) they will say   c) is they are going to say

5. … a long relationship? Yes, they will.

    a) They will have   b) Will they have   c) They are going to have

PART B

Write questions for each answer. Make sure that your question has the same verb tense as the answer.

> **EXAMPLE:** It will rain **tomorrow**.   Question: <u>When will it rain?</u>

6. Sam will live **in Paris**.

    Question: _____

7. They are going to travel **in 2025**.

    Question: _____

8. **Yes**, they will have children.

    Question: _____

9. Sam found a job **last year**.

    Question: _____

10. Sam likes his job **because his co-workers are friendly**.

    Question: _____

PART C

Underline and correct five errors in future tense forms.

won't

> **EXAMPLE:** Madam Salima <u>wont</u> read my palm.

Madam Salima is a fortune teller, and she makes many predictions. What the world will look like in ten years? According to Salima, people are gonna live in a very different world. The winters is going to be much warmer in Canada. Snow wont fall in some parts of the country. People are going to pay for water. Are we are going to reduce our water consumption?

WRITING

Work with a partner and tell each other about your future plans. Explain at least three things that you will do and at least three things that you won't do after you finish college. Then write a short paragraph describing your partner's future plans.

_____

_____

_____

_____

_____

_____

_____

_____

_____

_____

_____

_____

Past Progressive

Preview

WHAT IS THE PAST PROGRESSIVE?

The **past progressive** shows that a past action was interrupted or was in progress at a specific past time.

> *Yesterday, Daniel saw an accident while he **was driving** home.*
> *At 8 p.m., they **were studying**.*

ACCIDENT SCENE

Work with a partner. Examine the accident scene photo. Then do the following:

- Invent a name for each driver.
- Compose six sentences. Explain what happened. What was each driver doing when the accident occurred? Use your imagination!

_____

_____

_____

_____

_____

_____

_____

_____

_____

_____

_____

_____

Reading and Listening

IDENTIFY PAST PROGRESSIVE VERBS

Read the paragraph and guess what the missing past progressive verbs are. You can choose from the verbs below. On the Companion Website, listen to an audio recording of the reading. You can correct your answers.

| celebrate | hug | rest | stay |
| discuss | live | sleep | wait |

1. Malidoma Some was born in Burkina Faso, Africa. At the age of five, he

_____ in his bed when Jesuit missionaries took him away.

2. Fifteen years later, while he _____ in a Jesuit boarding school,

he rebelled and decided to return to his home village. **3.** He arrived home, but he

no longer knew his native tongue. While he _____ with his

parents, he relearned his language. **4.** One day, Malidoma arrived as the elders

_____ an initiation ceremony for adolescents. Malidoma asked

to do the ritual too. **5.** For six weeks, while the villagers _____,

twelve young males survived alone in the woods. **6.** One night, Malidoma

_____ near a tree when he had a vision. **7.** Later, the boys

returned to the village. While everyone _____, the elders

congratulated Malidoma. **8.** While his father _____ him,

Malidoma smiled. He felt like he belonged to his community.

Past Progressive: Forms and Usage

Use the past progressive in the following cases.

The past progressive indicates that **an action was in progress when another action happened or interrupted the first action**.

interruption

Last night, we **were sleeping when the phone rang**.

Last night the phone rang   **Now**

we **were sleeping**

The past progressive indicates that **an action was in progress at a specific past time**.

specific time
Last night, at **3:30 a.m.**, we **were sleeping**.

3:30 a.m.   **Now**
◄──►
we **were sleeping**

Key Words: as, when, while, at 3:30 a.m., at 10 p.m.

AFFIRMATIVE, QUESTION, AND NEGATIVE FORMS

AFFIRMATIVE FORM		QUESTION FORM (Move *be*.)		NEGATIVE FORM (Add *not*.)	
I She He It	**was** work**ing**.	**Was**	she work**ing**? he it	I She He It	**was not** work**ing**. (wasn't)
You We They	**were** work**ing**.	**Were**	you work**ing**? we they	You We They	**were not** work**ing**. (weren't)

NON-PROGRESSIVE VERBS

Some verbs, such as *understand, like, think,* and *believe*, are non-progressive. Refer to the chart of non-progressive verbs in Unit 3 on page 25.

                      wanted
Yesterday, during my performance, I ~~was wanting~~ to leave the stage.

For listening practice and for additional exercises, visit the Companion Website.

Practice

EXERCISE 1 PAST PROGRESSIVE

Fill in the blanks with the past progressive form of the verbs in parentheses.

    EXAMPLE: At that moment, a woman (sing) <u>was singing</u> quietly.

1. While I (walk) _____ past a large cathedral in Mexico City, I saw a large group of people.

2. At 2 p.m., the people (celebrate) _____ the Day of the Dead.

3. I noticed that people (wear) _____ traditional masks shaped like skulls.

4. While an old woman (place) _____ orange flowers on a grave, I took a photo of her.

5. As we (stand) _____ there, a woman explained that the flowers were called *ofrendas,* which means offerings.

6. We watched while families (build) _____ altars to the dead.

7. In the centre of the city, we heard music. We saw that people (dance) _____.

8. According to tradition, the dancers (try) _____ to wake up the dead with the noise from the shells on their costumes.

9. Fireworks lit up the sky while we (eat) _____.

10. While I (pay) _____ the bill, Juan left to see if he could buy some fireworks.

EXERCISE 2   NEGATIVE FORMS

Write the contracted negative form of the past progressive verbs.

    EXAMPLE: At 6 a.m., we (sleep, not) <u>weren't sleeping</u> .

1. Arturo (pay, not) _____ attention during the ceremony.

2. Eva and Anne (watch, not) _____ the prime minister.

3. They (pay, not) _____ attention the speech.

4. Arturo (wear, not) _____ a tie during the ceremony.

5. The citizens (listen, not) _____ when the politician discussed tax increases.

PAST PROGRESSIVE PROBLEMS

Don't use the past progressive to talk about past habits. Use the simple past.

    wrote
He ~~was writing~~ music when he was younger.

Don't use the past progressive to describe a series of past actions.

        played
When he was a child, he ~~was playing~~ the violin.

        went
Every night, he ~~was going~~ to his music teacher's house.

Don't overuse the past progressive! Only use this tense to emphasize that a past action was in progress.

EXERCISE 3 CONSIDER THE SITUATION

Read the pairs of sentences and then answer the questions that follow.

1. Don and Jason were saying their vows when the guests applauded.
    Sara and Kendra said their vows and the guests applauded.
    Which marriage ceremony was interrupted by applause? _____

2. When the ceremony ended, Simon left the room.
    When the ceremony ended, Alex was leaving the room.
    Who did not watch the end of the ceremony? _____

3. When Alex arrived, we ate.
    When Simon arrived, we were eating.
    Who missed part of the meal? _____

4. Nina left after Mark sang.
    Anne left while Mark was singing.
    Who listened to Mark's entire song? _____

5. While Nina was dancing, her baby cried.
    While Kelly was dancing, her baby was crying.
    Who ignored her crying baby? _____

EXERCISE 4 SIMPLE PAST AND PAST PROGRESSIVE

Underline the appropriate verb in parentheses.

    EXAMPLE: We (<u>flew</u> / were flying) to China on Air Canada.

1. My friends and I (went / was going) to China for the two-week-long New Year festivities.

2. Our friend Ellen (became / was becoming) our guide because she was the only one who could speak Mandarin.

3. I (didn't stay / wasn't staying) in Beijing for the whole trip.

4. While we (toured / were touring) Shanghai, a young girl approached us.

5. We bought a beautiful lantern that the child (sold / was selling).

6. One evening, while I (ate / was eating) noodles, I heard loud music outside.

7. I ran outside just as the festivities (began / were beginning).

8. We also (visited / were visiting) several other small villages.

9. While local women (built / were building) lanterns of paper and wood, I took photos.

10. Every night, some people (made / were making) lanterns.

11. While Ellen and I (watched / were watching) a parade, it started to rain.

12. We (took / were taking) a train back to Beijing.

SIMPLE PAST AND PAST PROGRESSIVE

Fill in the blanks with the simple past or the past progressive.

> **EXAMPLE:** The bulls (enter) _entered_ the streets while hundreds of people (run) _were running_ away from them.

1. On July 7th at 7 a.m., I (sleep) _____ when the alarm clock suddenly (ring) _____. That morning, many people (want) _____ to run with the bulls.

2. While my friend Pablo (register) _____ for the event, I interrupted him. I asked if he really wanted to run with the bulls. Pablo (say) _____, "Absolutely."

3. We entered a restaurant and (order) _____ breakfast. Someone (fall) _____ on the slippery floor while we (eat) _____.

4. About twenty minutes later, while we (pay) _____ the bill, a man grabbed Pablo's arm. Together, they (leave) _____ to take their starting positions.

5. Later, I realized that people (cheer) _____. I quickly (run) _____ outside.

6. While people (run) _____ past me, I looked for Pablo.

7. Then I (see) _____ Pablo in the distance. I (scream) _____ because a bull (run) _____ towards Pablo.

8. That night, while we (watch) _____ the news on television, we (see) _____ Pablo with the bulls.

EXERCISE 6 **IDENTIFY ERRORS**

Correct nine errors in the underlined verbs. Write *C* above five correct verbs.

> didn't stop
> **EXAMPLE:** Last night, my taxi driver <u>wasn't stopping</u> at the red lights.

1. While I <u>walking</u> to the beach, I <u>saw</u> a beautiful Greek wedding.

2. A taxi almost hit us while we <u>were cross</u> the street.

3. I <u>wasn't understanding</u> why guests <u>were attaching</u> money to the bride's dress.

TIP

Non-Progressive Verbs

Some verbs are rarely in the *–ing* form. For example, you should not say, *He was wanting food.* For a list of some common non-progressive verbs, see Unit 3, page 25.

4. I asked another guest about the tradition, but he <u>wasn't hearing</u> me.

5. We <u>were deciding</u> **to crash*** the wedding.

6. A firecracker <u>was exploding</u> while we <u>were drinking</u> some wine.

7. People ate, and then they <u>danced</u>.

8. The bride and groom kissed and then <u>were giving</u> each guest a gift.

9. A limousine <u>arrived</u> while we <u>was dancing</u>.

10. The ceremony was beautiful, and I <u>was loving</u> it.

———————

* to crash: to attend without an invitation

WHILE OR DURING?

Do not confuse *while* and *during*. Notice the difference in meaning.

While refers to a period of time and is followed by a subject and verb. Use **while** in sentences with two actions.

              verb   verb
While Teresa <u>was cooking</u>, she <u>burned</u> her finger.

     verb   verb
*We <u>saw</u> a deer **while** we <u>were driving</u> to Banff.*

During is a preposition and is followed by a noun. Use **during** to refer to a specific event.

             noun
During <u>the movie</u>, I fell asleep.

                      noun
*Many soldiers died **during** <u>the war</u>.*

EXERCISE 7 *WHILE* OR *DURING*

Add *while* or *during* to each sentence.

    EXAMPLE: <u>During</u> weddings, some people become emotional.

1. Last year, _____ Justin was shopping for a wedding gift, he lost his wallet.

2. What did you do _____ the ceremony?

3. The groom waited _____ the bride was putting on her dress.

4. _____ the banquet, the best man made a speech.

5. _____ the people were dancing, the lights suddenly went out.

6. What did the people do _____ the blackout?

7. Rebeka ran outside _____ the organ music was playing.

8. _____ the honeymoon, the couple had a big fight.

EXERCISE 8 QUESTION FORMS

Add an auxiliary to the questions below. The question may be in the present or past. Choose from the following auxiliaries.

is   are   do   does   did   was   were

EXAMPLE: When _does_ the guest of honour arrive?

1. _____ you sometimes go to special ceremonies?

2. When _____ the ceremony usually begin?

3. Yesterday, why _____ the fifteen-year-old Mexican girl have a party?

4. Why _____ the young men wearing suits?

5. Yesterday at 2 p.m., what _____ the old woman doing?

6. Last night, why _____ the music suddenly stop?

7. Yesterday, what _____ the girl do after the party?

8. What _____ your opinion about initiations?

9. Why _____ some cultures have special initiation ceremonies?

SUBJECT QUESTIONS

When *who*, *what*, and *how many* ask about the <u>subject</u> of a question, no auxiliary is needed.

Dora broke the law.	*Her car* was blue.	*Five people* were hurt.
↑	↑	↑
Who broke the law?	*What* was blue?	*How many people* were hurt?

EXERCISE 9 MIXED TENSES

Write questions for the following sentences. The answers are in bold.

EXAMPLE: Eliana received *a watch*.   <u>What did Eliana receive</u>?

1. Eliana had a birthday **on February 12th**.

_____

2. She was **fifteen years** old.

_____

3. She was walking **to her party** when the police stopped her.

_____

4. **The police officer** was very serious.

   _____

5. The event happened **last Friday**.

   _____

6. She received **a ticket for jaywalking**.

   _____

7. She asked **the officer** for another chance.

   _____

8. He refused **because jaywalking is illegal**.

   _____

9. She paid **$70**.

   _____

10. **Eliana** was unhappy.

   _____

↺ UNIT Review

Answer the following questions. If you don't know an answer, go back and review the appropriate section.

1. When do you use the past progressive?

   _____

   _____

2. Underline and correct the verb errors in the sentences below. Then explain why the sentences are incorrect.

   a) Every day, he was walking to school. _____

   Reason: _____

   b) While I eat, the phone rang. _____

   Reason: _____

3. Write the question and negative forms of the following sentences.

   a) She turned on the radio.

   Question: _____

   Negative: _____

   b) They were eating when the phone rang.

   Question: _____

   Negative: _____

Need more practice?
Visit the Companion Website and try additional past progressive exercises.

78 | AVENUES 1 | English Grammar

Final Review

PART A

Underline the correct verb.

> **EXAMPLE:** In 2006, my sister (<u>was working</u> / working) in London when she met her future husband.

1. When I (was / was being) still a teenager, my older sister Lola (married / was marrying) a man from Germany named Gunther.

2. We (did not know / were not knowing) that Germans have specific wedding traditions.

3. When (they started / did they start / were they starting) the "plate smashing" ritual?

4. The night before the wedding, while I (eating / was eating / ate) in the kitchen, I suddenly (was hearing / heard) a loud sound.

5. I went into the hall. I watched while some friends (were throwing / threw) plates on the floor. I (wasn't understanding / didn't understand) why they were doing it.

6. Then somebody (explained / was explaining) the tradition to me. At German weddings, friends of the couple break many plates. Then the bride and groom (clean / cleaning / were cleaning) up the mess. It is a German tradition to prove that the bride and groom work well together.

7. Later, while Lola and her fiancé (cleaned / were cleaning) up the mess, some people applauded.

8. That evening, the groom's friends entered the couple's bedroom and (put / were putting) many alarm clocks under the bed.

9. On their wedding night, at 5 a.m., while my sister and her husband (slept / were sleeping) peacefully, some alarm clocks suddenly started to beep.

10. The noise (was waking / woke) Lola up. She (didn't like / wasn't liking) the alarm clock tradition!

PART B

Write yes/no questions for the following sentences.

    EXAMPLE: The celebration was fun. <u>Was the celebration fun?</u>

11. Their friends were nice.

_____

12. The wedding lasted for three days.

_____

13. Lola was smiling in the photo.

_____

14. She enjoyed the ceremony.

_____

15. They stayed in Germany for a month.

_____

WRITING

Write about a significant ceremony or event that you witnessed. You can write about a birth, a wedding, a birthday, a religious holiday, or a funeral.

Describe where you were when the event happened. What were you doing? Write six to ten sentences. Include simple past and past progressive verbs. Also include at least one negative form and one question.

_____

_____

_____

_____

_____

_____

_____

_____

_____

_____

_____

_____

_____

Prepositions

Preview

WHAT ARE PREPOSITIONS?

Prepositions are short words that show connections between ideas. They can indicate time, place, or direction, and they usually appear before a noun or pronoun.

In the afternoon, I went to the mall with my sister. She lives beside me.
We walked through many stores. We stayed at the mall for three hours.

GIVE DIRECTIONS

Work with a partner and choose one of the following locations:

bookstore	coffee shop	bank
cafeteria	library	shopping mall

Imagine that a visitor is in the room. The visitor wants to go to that place. Write a short paragraph with very specific directions. Explain how to get to the location that you chose. You can use the following vocabulary in your directions.

across from	below	down	through
above	beside	inside/outside	up

_____

_____

_____

_____

_____

_____

_____

_____

_____

_____

Reading and Listening

IDENTIFY PREPOSITIONS

Read the paragraph and guess what the missing prepositions are. Write your choices in the blanks. On the Companion Website, listen to an audio recording of the reading. You can correct your answers.

1. Kristin Riddick, in her book *Barbie: The Image of Us All*, describes the history _____ the Barbie doll. **2.** _____ Barbie, most dolls looked like babies. **3.** But Mattel's new toy was different _____ other dolls. **4.** The idea came to Ruth Handler when she saw her daughter playing _____ paper dolls. **5.** She watched her daughter _____ ten minutes and then had an inspiration. **6.** Girls love _____ dress paper dolls, but would they also love real "women" dolls?

7. _____ a trip to Germany, another event reinforced her idea. **8.** She saw a shapely doll _____ a toy fair. **9.** The Lilli doll, _____ a small waist and a large chest, was based on a German comic strip character. **10.** _____ 1958, Handler designed the first Barbie doll.

11. The next year, Mattel sold the first Barbies _____ a toy fair.

12. People paid $3 _____ their dolls, and the toys were very popular.

Prepositions: Forms and Usage

PREPOSITIONS OF TIME AND PLACE

The prepositions *in*, *on*, *at*, *from ... to*, and *for* indicate a general or precise time or place.

	PREPOSITIONS OF TIME		PREPOSITIONS OF PLACE	
in	**in** a year **in** a month **in** the morning/afternoon/evening **in** a season	**in** 2005 **in** February **in** the summer	**in** a city **in** a country **in** a continent	**in** Calgary **in** Japan **in** Africa
on	**on** a day of the week **on** a specific date **on** a specific holiday **on** time (meaning "punctual")	**on** Tuesday **on** January 25th **on** Labour Day **on** my birthday	**on** a specific street **on** a planet **on** a technological device **on** top	**on** Main Street **on** Earth **on** TV/the radio/ the phone/ the computer
at	**at** a specific time of day **at** night **at** breakfast, lunch, dinner	**at** 1:30	**at** a specific address **at** a specific building	**at** 32 Elm Avenue **at** the hotel

Continued	PREPOSITIONS OF TIME		PREPOSITIONS OF PLACE	
from ... to	**from** one time **to** another	**from** 9 a.m. **to** 6 p.m.	**from** one place **to** another	**from** Chile **to** Canada
for	**for** a period of time	**for** two hours	**for** a distance	**for** five kilometres

Generally, as a description of a place or time becomes more precise, you move from *in* to *on* to *at*.

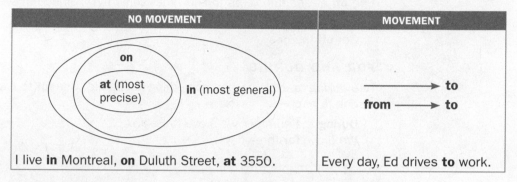

NO MOVEMENT	MOVEMENT
on · at (most precise) · in (most general)	⟶ to · from ⟶ to
I live **in** Montreal, **on** Duluth Street, **at** 3550.	Every day, Ed drives **to** work.

PREPOSITIONS OF PLACE

Study the meaning of the following prepositions:

above	below	between	near	outside
against	beneath	in front of	next to	over
behind	beside	inside	on/on top of	under

The cat is **on** the box.
The cat is **on top of** the box.

The cat is **next to** the box.
The cat is **beside** the box.

The bird is **above** the box.
The box is **below** the bird.
The box is **under** the bird.

The box is **against** the wall.

The cat is **behind** the box.
The box is **in front of** the cat.

The cat is **between** the boxes.

FROM, OF, AND OFF

Use *from* to show that something originated at a particular point.

He is **from** Halifax. He graduated **from** Oakville High School.

Use *of* to show that something is part of a larger group. Also use *of* to show the composition of an object.

He is at the top **of** his class. The trophy is made **of** glass and steel.

Use *off* after some verbs to show that something will be removed.

Please take **off** your shoes in my house.
Get **off** the bus.

FOR AND DURING

Use *during* to explain when something happened. Use *for* to explain how long it took to happen.

During the summer, we drove to Halifax.
We drove **for** three days.

Practice

For listening practice and for additional exercises, visit the Companion Website.

EXERCISE 1 PREPOSITIONS OF TIME AND PLACE

Write *in*, *on*, or *at* in the spaces provided.

EXAMPLE: _in_ November

1. _____ the morning		8. _____ September	
2. _____ the phone		9. _____ the winter	
3. _____ 32 Ocean Drive		10. _____ March 12th	
4. _____ Spain		11. _____ midnight	
5. _____ Pine Avenue		12. _____ television	
6. _____ 1994		13. _____ June	
7. _____ night		14. _____ my birthday	

EXERCISE 2 PREPOSITIONS OF TIME AND PLACE

Fill in the blanks with appropriate prepositions of time and place. You can use *in, on, at, for,* or *from … to.*

EXAMPLE: The champion was born _in_ Canada.

1. Many young people enjoy trading-card games. _____ 1960, the first collectible trading-card game arrived on the market. Math professor Richard Garfield created the game, and _____ 1991 _____ 1993, he produced it with a company called Wizards of the Coast. _____ Whitman College, _____ Boyer Avenue _____ Walla Walla, Washington, Garfield tested the game with some of his math students.

2. Magic: The Gathering became very successful in a short time. The game was introduced at the annual Gen Con gaming convention _____ Milwaukee _____ 1993. The event was in the convention centre _____ 226 West Kilbourne Avenue. Players competed _____ ten hours.

3. Wizards of the Coast sold out their whole stock of 2.5 million cards, which was supposed to last _____ the time of the convention _____ the end of 1993. _____ August 19, 1994, the first Magic World Championship was held _____ Milwaukee. People drove _____ many kilometres to compete.

4. Nobody received prize money _____ the World Championship, but winner Zak Dolan received many valuable cards. Today, people receive large prizes _____ different Magic Card tournaments.

5. _____ June 1st, _____ 1994, Garfield decided to design games full-time. Garfield practised his games _____ the morning, _____ noon, and _____ the evening. Garfield earned millions of dollars from the game, and Magic created a boom in trading-card games _____ 1994 _____ the present day.

EXERCISE 3 PREPOSITIONS OF PLACE

Fill in the blanks with one of the following prepositions. Use each preposition only once. Cross it off the list after you use it.

above	below	between	on
behind	beside	in front of	under

1. In the living room, the fireplace is _____ the picture.

2. Or, to put it another way, the picture is _____ the fireplace.
The fireplace is _____ two windows. A small plant is _____ the glass table.

3. The glass table is _____ the beige sofa. A tall plant is _____ the blue chair.
The rug is _____ the glass table. The tall plant is _____ the window.

> ### TO AND AT
>
> Use **to** after verbs that indicate movement from one place to another.
>
> go **to**   move **to**   return **to**   run **to**   walk **to**
>
> **Exception:** Don't put *to* directly before *home*.
>
> I'll go ~~to~~ home with you.   I won't go to his home.
>
> Use **at** after verbs that indicate stillness.
>
> meet **at**   sit **at**   stay **at**   wait **at**   work **at**

EXERCISE 4 TO AND AT

Write *at, to,* or *X* in the spaces provided. Note that *X* means no preposition is needed.

> **EXAMPLE:** This week, the boss is staying _at_ the Ritz Hotel in Vancouver.

1. Every summer, many tourists come _____ Montreal to see the comedy or jazz festivals. They stay _____ local hotels and they go _____ restaurants and museums.

2. For example, Mr. Steve Winland is from Toronto. He works _____ a hospital. He drives _____ Montreal every July. He goes _____ comedy clubs. Then he goes _____ home one week later. Next summer, he will go _____ Montreal again. Sometimes, he says that he would like to move _____ Montreal.

EXERCISE 5 FOR AND DURING

Fill in the blanks with *for* or *during*.

> **EXAMPLE:** _During_ the summer of 1976, he lived in Africa.

1. In 1976, Charles Gaines was in Africa _____ six weeks. _____ his trip, he hunted large animals. A few months later, _____ a poker game, he described the excitement of the hunt to his friend, Hayes Noel. They decided to invent a game in which people could shoot one another with balls of paint. They worked on their idea _____ five years.

2. _____ the summer of 1980, the paintball fad began. _____ three years, the sport grew in popularity, and more companies developed paintball guns. One day, in 1984, Karen Isackson damaged her retina _____ a game. After that, paintball players had to follow very strict safety rules. Whether the game lasts _____ ten minutes or five hours, the players must wear goggles and protective clothing.

TIP

For and **During**

During an event:
During the war, Josh had many bad experiences.

For a period of time:
He stayed in Afghanistan **for** two years.

INFINITIVE FORM

The infinitive consists of *to* and the base form of the verb. Never use *for* in infinitive forms, and never put *for* and *to* together.

>   **to**
> She is ready ~~for to~~ buy a car.

EXERCISE 6 IDENTIFY ERRORS

Underline and correct the preposition errors. There may be more than one error in each sentence. If necessary, review the preposition rules at the beginning of this unit.

                                             for
EXAMPLE: Elaine and I went dancing <u>during</u> three hours.

1. When Carlos was a child, he sang and danced for to get attention.

2. Later, he studied dramatic arts during three years.

3. On 2009, he got a role in a Canadian movie.

4. During the filming, he moved in Vancouver during three weeks.

5. He felt lonely because he was very far of his family.

6. He worked really hard for make his character seem believable.

7. One day, during an important scene, there was no electricity during three hours.

8. Carlos returned at Montreal on June 25th because he didn't have a good reason for stay in Vancouver.

9. Last week, Carlos received a telephone call of his agent, and now he has many job offers.

10. He is ready for to become a serious actor.

TIP

Finance-Related Expressions

Pay **for**:   When you buy something, you pay **for** it.

Spend money **on**:   You spend money **on** something.
> *I will pay <u>**for**</u> the tickets. You don't have to spend money <u>**on**</u> them.*

EXERCISE 7 CHOOSE THE CORRECT PREPOSITION

Underline the correct prepositions in parentheses below. Note that *X* means nothing is required.

1. (On / At / In) 1979, some Canadians invented a popular board game called Trivial Pursuit. Players start with a "pie" that they must fill (X / whit / with) triangular pie pieces. They must correctly answer a trivia question. The game also comes (X / whit / with) many question cards.

2. (In / On / At) 1994, (in / on / at) a Nova Scotia courthouse, a man named David Wall sued the creators of Trivial Pursuit. He says he hitchhiked in a car (X / whit / with) Trivial Pursuit co-creator Chris Haney. They were on a trip (at / to / X) Sydney, Nova Scotia. Wall says that they talked about a trivia board game (for / at / during) the trip.

3. (On / During / For) the next thirteen years, the case was argued in several different courts. Reporters talked about the case (in / on / at) television and (in / on / at) the radio. Haney claimed that he had drawings of a game resembling Trivial Pursuit. However, he did not bring any drawings (at / on / to) court. (In / On / At) June 5th, 2007, (on / at / in) 3 p.m., the Nova Scotia Supreme Court ruled in favour of Trivial Pursuit's creators. The judge said that Wall was not credible.

4. I love Trivial Pursuit, and I recently received an updated game. I didn't pay (X / for) it. Instead, my friend spent $30 (in / on / at) the game. We play (for / on) many hours every weekend.

↻ UNIT Review

Answer the following questions. If you don't know an answer, go back and review the appropriate section.

1. Write *in, on,* or *at* in the spaces provided.

   a) _____ 1995   d) _____ March 15th   g) _____ the phone

   b) _____ 5 p.m.   e) _____ Mexico   h) _____ Vancouver

   c) _____ night   f) _____ TV   i) _____ Elm Road

2. Write *for* or *during* in the spaces provided.

   I watched the movie _____ three hours. _____ the movie, my cellphone rang. I left the room, and I spoke on the phone _____ about three minutes.

3. Which preposition follows the verbs *go, run,* and *walk*?   a) to   b) at

4. Which preposition follows the verbs *sit, wait,* and *stay*?   a) to   b) at

Final Review

PART A

Underline the correct prepositions in parentheses below. Note that *X* means no preposition is needed.

    EXAMPLE: (On / At / <u>In</u>) 1971, the first video game was released to the public.

1. *Computer Space* was the first video game. It was an arcade game that was played (X / whit / with) coins. Customers could play the game (on / at / in) the afternoon. There was a video arcade (in / on / at) Green Avenue, and many people gathered there.

Early video game player

2. The game *Pong* was popular (from / to / at) 1974 (to / from / after) 1976. Some people paid (X / for / to) the inexpensive consoles. They could play the game (for / during) hours. My father played every day (for / during) his lunch hour. He had to return to work (in / on / at) 1 p.m., so he played (for / from / during) thirty minutes. Eventually, Atari made over $20 million from *Pong* sales.

3. *Pac-Man* was released (in / on / at) Japan (in / on / at) May 22, 1980. While most video games were popular (with / whit / wiht) males, *Pac-Man* also appealed to females. The game was simple. A little blue head ate dots and fruit. My mother sometimes went (X / at / to) the video arcade to play *Pac-Man*.

4. Finally, another Japanese company decided (to / on / at) develop video games. Nintendo was not originally a game company. (In / On / At) September, 1889, it opened as a card company. Then (during / for / at) several years, (for / during / at) the 1930s, it was a taxi company. Finally, in the 1970s, Nintendo made video games. (In / On / At) March 10, 1977, the company announced the release of the Nintendo Entertainment System. People could put the system (of / between / under) their televisions.

PART B

Underline and correct the preposition error in each sentence. Write *C* beside correct sentences.

                                       from

    EXAMPLE: Terrel received a call <u>of</u> his mother.

5. In the 1990s, Terrel Wayne loved *Super Mario*, and he often played it whit his friends.

6. Terrel played the game for over twenty hours each week.

7. Terrel worked really hard for to do well in his courses.

8. Often, he spent his money in a new game.

9. *Super Mario* was a popular game during many years.

 **WRITING**

Draw a picture or map of your favourite room. This could be a room in your house, or it could be a room in a public place (restaurant, coffee shop, etc.). Then write a descriptive paragraph about that room. Use prepositions to explain where items are.

EXAMPLE: The clock is ***above*** the sofa.

Modal Auxiliaries

UNIT 9

Preview

WHAT ARE MODAL AUXILIARIES?

Modal auxiliaries are a special class of words that indicate functions, attitude, and mood. Modals have no third-person singular form.

Compare: *Vince **builds** products.*   *Vince **can build** homes.*

THE SKYDIVER

Work with a partner. Complete the sentences below by adding one of the following modals. Use each modal only once.

| can | will | would | should | ~~can't~~ | might | must |

1.
I ____**can't**____ do it!
I'm too scared!

4.
I suppose I _____
do it.
I paid $200 for the course.

2.
My parachute _____
not open.

5.
I promised myself that
I _____ do it!
I think I _____ do it!

3.
You _____ go out
there.
It is safe, and you
_____ be fine!

6.
Yes! I am doing it!

Reading and Listening

IDENTIFY MODALS

Read the paragraph and add the missing modal auxiliaries. Write your choices in the blanks. On the Companion Website, listen to an audio recording of the reading. You can correct your answers.

1. When I was a child, I knew that I _____ travel one day.

2. I thought that I _____ visit every country in the world.

3. Now, I am more realistic. I _____ be happy to visit ten countries.

4. Everyone_____ travel because there are so many benefits.

5. Before you travel to another country, there are things you _____ do.

6. First, you _____ get a passport.

7. People _____ apply for a passport online.

8. Then you _____ bring your birth certificate to a passport office.

9. You _____ find out if you need special vaccines.

10. You _____ learn a lot about yourself when you travel.

Modal Auxiliaries: Forms and Usage

Review the list of common modals.

COMMON MODAL AUXILIARIES			
Modal	Function	Example	Negative
can	ability possibility	She **can speak** English. We **can leave** together.	**cannot** (can't)
could	past ability possibility	She **could speak** Greek when she was young. You **could stay** here. We have a spare bedroom.	**could not** (couldn't)
may	possibility polite request	We **may go** to Nova Scotia. **May** I **help** you? (used with *I* or *we* to ask permission)	**may not**
might	possibility	Maggie **might take** the job in Halifax.	**might not**
should	advice	She **should see** a lawyer.	**should not** (shouldn't)
must	obligation probability	We **must show** identification at the airport. It **must be** cold in Yellowknife.	**must not** (mustn't)
have to*	obligation	You **have to bring** your passport. The child **has to travel** with an adult.	**do not have to** (don't) **does not have to** (doesn't)

*Although *have to* isn't a modal auxiliary, it is included on this list because it functions like a modal and has the same meaning as *must*. For question and negative forms, you must add *do* or *does*. *Does he have to leave? He doesn't have to leave.*

Continued

COMMON MODAL AUXILIARIES			
Modal	**Function**	**Example**	**Negative**
will	prediction willingness	He **will use** his credit card. I **will answer** the door.	**will not** (won't)
would	desire condition past habit preference (used with *rather*)	I **would like** to travel in first class. I **would go** to Italy if I had the money. When I was a child, I **would walk** everywhere. I **would rather drive** than fly.	**would not** (wouldn't)

Practice

EXERCISE 1 IDENTIFY MODAL FUNCTIONS

Identify the functions of the underlined modals. You can use the following words to help you.

ability (AB)   advice (AD)   desire (D)   obligation (O)   possibility (P)

EXAMPLE: People <u>should discipline</u> their children.   <u>AD</u>

1. Some parents <u>may use</u> a time out as a disciplining method. _____

2. Children <u>can learn</u> to share. _____

3. You <u>must stop</u> screaming at that child! _____

4. Some children <u>might be</u> more difficult than others. _____

5. Every parent <u>would like</u> to be a positive role model. _____

6. When your son behaves well, you <u>should reward</u> him. _____

7. The boy <u>must listen</u> to his mother. _____

8. She <u>should never hit</u> her child. _____

NEGATIVE FORMS OF MODALS

Look at the negative forms of the following modals. Notice that when you add *not* to *can*, it becomes one word. You can contract the negative forms of most modals.

should not	could not	would not	must not	**cannot**
shouldn't	couldn't	wouldn't	mustn't	can't

EXERCISE 2 NEGATIVE FORMS

PART A

Write the following modal auxiliaries in their contracted negative forms.

EXAMPLE: can   can't

1. would   _____
2. can   _____
3. should   _____

4. could   _____
5. have to   _____
6. has to   _____

PART B

Write the negative form of the modals and verbs. Do *not* use contractions.

EXAMPLE: I **should wear** a hat today.   should not wear

7. People **should take** risks.   _____

8. You **can ride** a bike on the sand.   _____

9. We **would like** to stay near the ocean.   _____

10. I **must quit** my job.   _____

TIP

Would and *Could*

When you tell a story about a past event: use **would** instead of *will*
                                          use **could** instead of *can*.

would   could
*Last, summer, I knew that I ~~will~~ take a Spanish course. I believed that I ~~can~~
succeed. Sure enough, I got an A in my class.* ·

EXERCISE 3 PRESENT AND PAST FORMS

Underline the correct modal auxiliary. Choose a past or present form.

EXAMPLE: When Mawlid was young, his parents (can / <u>could</u>) leave him alone
because the villagers cared for him. Most children in Canada (<u>can't</u> / couldn't)
travel around their cities alone.

1. Mawlid is from Somalia. When he was a child, he (can / could) go anywhere in
his village alone. Family members and friends (will / would) take care of him.
However, he (can't / couldn't) show any disrespect to his elders or the villagers
(will / would) reject him.

2. Today, children in Canada (can / could) speak quite freely. For example, if ten-year-old Kara feels angry tomorrow, she (will / would) probably yell at her mother. But when Mawlid was a child, he (will / would) never shout at his parents.

3. Mawlid grew up in the middle of a civil war in Somalia. When he was fourteen, he (can't / couldn't) stay in Somalia any longer, so he escaped to Ethiopia. His mother told Mawlid that he (will / would) be safer in another country.

4. These days, Mawlid lives in Montreal with his children. His daughter (can / could) go to school alone. She is only six years old, and she (can / could) read and write. At her school, the teachers (can't / couldn't) hit the children. Next year, she (will / would) enter a private school.

POLITE REQUESTS

May, would, could, and *can* express different levels of requests from formal, or most polite, to informal.

Most polite	**May**	*May* I help you? (Use *may* with the pronoun *I* or *we*.)
↓	**Would**	*Would* you like some coffee?
	Could	*Could* you pass the salt?
Informal	**Can**	*Can* I borrow your eraser? (Use *can* with family and friends. Use more polite forms with strangers.)

EXERCISE 4 CHOOSE MODALS

Write *may, would, could,* or *can* in the blanks. Sometimes more than one choice is acceptable.

1. Teacher: _____ I speak with you in private?

2. Parent: Well, _____ you explain what is going on? Why _____ you like to see me?

3. Teacher: There is a problem. _____ you like to sit down? Your daughter copied her exam from another student.

   _____ you please look at these two exams?

4. Parent: Oh, I can see the problem. _____ I keep a copy of the exam? I _____ like to discuss this with my daughter.

5. Teacher: Of course. _____ you like any more information?

MUST NOT AND *DON'T HAVE TO*

Both *must* and *have to* indicate that something is necessary. (*You must finish your homework. You have to finish soon.*) However, the meanings are different in the negative form.

Must not means "it is not permitted."

You **must not work** *today. You are too sick, and you are contagious.*

Don't have to means "there is no obligation, but you can do it if you want."

You **don't have to stay** *in bed. You can watch TV if you prefer.*

EXERCISE 5 WRITE NEGATIVE FORMS

Fill in the blanks with *must not*, *don't have to*, or *doesn't have to*.

EXAMPLE: In Japan, you _don't have to_ shake hands when you meet someone.

1. In Canada, you _____ call someone *sir* or *madam*. However, you can use those terms if you want to show respect.

2. People _____ smoke inside government buildings. It is illegal.

3. When you travel within Canada, you _____ show your passport. But if you go across the border, you will need it.

4. When you travel across borders, you _____ bring a gun with you. It is against the law.

5. Kamal can go to the United States if she wants, but she _____ go. She can stay here.

PRESENT AND PAST OBLIGATION

Must and *have to* indicate a present obligation. *Had to* indicates a past obligation.

present	present	past
I **have to leave**.	I **must work** tonight.	I **had to work** last night, too.

EXERCISE 6 PRESENT AND PAST OBLIGATION

Write the appropriate modals in the spaces provided. Note that in some sentences, more than one answer is possible.

EXAMPLE: Kids (advice) _should_ take some risks.
They (necessity) _must_ learn to be independent.

1. Fred and Elisa (desire) _____ like to adopt a baby. To adopt a child,

   parents (obligation) _____ pass certain tests. Last year, Fred and

Elisa (past obligation) _____ visit a psychologist. These days, they (ability, not) _____ find a child in Nova Scotia. Maybe they (advise) _____ try to adopt an older child.

2. Most teenagers (obligation) _____ live with their parents. They (ability, not) _____ leave home. When I was a teenager, I (past obligation) _____ live with my parents. However, some parents give their children a lot of freedom. In 2009, sixteen-year-old Abby Sunderland decided to sail around the world alone. Unfortunately, she (past obligation) _____ ask for help. A fishing boat (past obligation) _____ rescue Abby.

3. Most parents (desire) _____ like to raise adventurous children. Perhaps parents (advice) _____ follow the example of Abby's parents. They (advice) _____ not overprotect their children. Most children (ability) _____ act responsibly.

QUESTION FORMS

To form a question, move the modal before the subject.

They can swim.	**Can** *they swim?*
She should leave.	**Should** *she leave?*

Have to is a regular verb. You must add an auxiliary (*do, does, did*) to the question form.

Henry has to work late.	**Does** *he* **have to** *work late?*

EXERCISE 7 WRITE QUESTIONS

Write questions. The answers are in bold.

    EXAMPLE: He should leave ***tomorrow***. <u>When should he leave?</u>

1. Alex can stay in Japan **for three weeks**.

_____

2. He should bring **an umbrella**.

_____

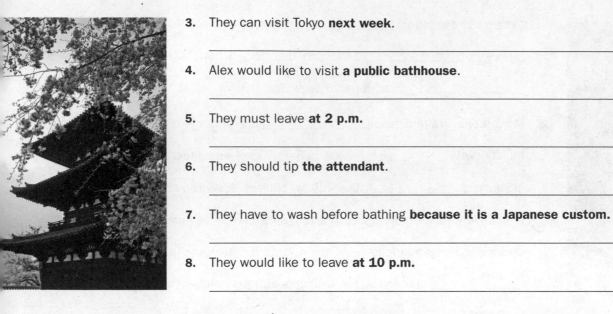

3. They can visit Tokyo **next week**.

_____

4. Alex would like to visit **a public bathhouse**.

_____

5. They must leave **at 2 p.m.**

_____

6. They should tip **the attendant**.

_____

7. They have to wash before bathing **because it is a Japanese custom.**

_____

8. They would like to leave **at 10 p.m.**

_____

COMMON MODAL PROBLEMS

When you use modals, avoid the following errors.

Never place two modal auxiliaries together.

We ~~can~~ should finish the project together.

Use the base form of the verb that follows the modal. Don't place _to_ between the modal auxiliary and the verb and don't use the _–ing_ form of the verb.

You must ~~to~~ help us. We should work~~ing~~ together.

Never write _gotta_.

Gotta is often heard in spoken English. However, it isn't a word and should never be written. Get into the habit of using _have to_ instead of _got to_ or _gotta_.

   have to
I ~~gotta~~ finish this report.

EXERCISE 8 IDENTIFY ERRORS

Correct the errors in the underlined modals and verbs. Write _C_ next to correct sentences.

    EXAMPLE: Kids <u>must to learn</u> independence at a young age.   <u>must learn</u>

1. According to Lenore Skenazy, children <u>must taking</u> some chances.   _____

2. In the 1960s, young children <u>can walk</u> to school alone, but today most children cannot.   _____

3. In 2008, Skenazy's ten-year-old son <u>has to</u> take the subway home.   _____

4. He took the subway alone, and he said that he <u>would be</u> careful. _____

5. A newspaper reporter criticized Skenazy: "New York is a dangerous place, and children <u>must not travelling</u> alone!" _____

6. Skenazy knew that her decision <u>will be</u> controversial. _____

7. At what age <u>kids can explore</u> on their own? _____

8. According to Skenazy, parents <u>should to relax</u>. _____

9. Children <u>gotta learn</u> to be independent. _____

10. <u>Do you could</u> travel alone when you were a child? _____

↻ UNIT   Review

Answer the following questions. If you don't know an answer, go back and review the appropriate section.

1. Which modals mean "ability"? _____

2. Underline the three modals that express possibility. Circle the modal that expresses advice.

   could   have to   may   might   must   should

3. Underline the negative modal form that means "it isn't an obligation."

   must not   don't have to

4. Correct the errors in the following sentences. Then write a rule about each error.

   a) You shouldn't eating too fast. _____

   Rule: _____

   b) Do you can cook something? _____

   Rule: _____

   c) We should to work together. _____

   Rule: _____

Need more practice?
Visit the Companion Website and try additional exercises about modals.

Final Review

© PEARSON LONGMAN • REPRODUCTION PROHIBITED

PART A

Circle the letter of the best answer.

1. I … with Amanda right away. I have no choice. It is urgent.

    a) can speak b) may speak c) must speak

2. When she was a teenager, in the 1980s, Amanda … children every weekend.

    a) will babysit b) would babysit c) can babysit

3. Now Amanda … to adopt a child. It is her greatest desire.

    a) would like b) would likes c) should like

4. Where … a baby to adopt?

    a) she can find b) do she can find c) can she find

5. Last year, she … a baby in this province because no babies were available.

    a) can't adopt b) couldn't adopt c) don't can adopt

6. She … for a child overseas.

    a) may to look b) might look c) can looking

7. Where …?

    a) she should go b) she should goes c) should she go

8. Amanda … in China. It is too expensive to adopt there.

    a) can't search b) can't to search c) can't searching

9. Last year, she lost her job. She … a much lower-paying job.

    a) had to take b) has to took c) had to took

10. She will be a great mother. She … an orphan a better life.

    a) can to give b) can giving c) can give

PART B

Identify and correct five errors in the underlined verbs. Write *C* above two correct verbs.

11. There are some controversies surrounding adoptions. People from rich countries <u>can taking</u> children from poor countries. People <u>can go</u> to Africa and adopt children who have living parents. For example, Madonna's son David is from Malawi. David is not an orphan, but in 2006, David's father <u>couldn't supported</u> the boy. He <u>had to gave</u> away his son. <u>Should celebrities should adopt</u> children who are not orphans? Maybe they <u>should giving</u> money to the poor families instead? On the other hand, Madonna <u>can provide</u> a very good life for her adopted children. It is a complex issue.

 **WRITING** Work with a partner, and read the following letters and e-mails. Discuss what each letter writer should do. Then write letters of advice to two of the writers.

I really want to be a famous actor or singer, but I could not get into my college's theatre or music department. What should I do? Should I move to Hollywood, California and try to become famous? I don't have much money, but I am sure I will succeed. What should I do? Muriel

My son Jordan is twenty-five years old. He doesn't have a job, and he doesn't go to school. He's very lazy, and he never helps around the house. My wife thinks we should kick Jordan out. What should we do?
Antonio

Last week, when I visited my friends, something bad happened. Ben, their five-year-old son, was very annoying. He sat on me and pulled my hair, and his parents didn't react. I shouted at the boy, and I spanked his bottom. Now my friends are angry with me. Was I wrong?

Raul

I'm sixteen years old, and I'm very lonely. I am very shy and cannot meet people easily. Recently, I met a nice guy on the Internet. He's nineteen, and he lives in another city. He wants to send me a bus ticket to visit him. Should I go?

Alexandra

_____

_____

_____

_____

_____

_____

_____

_____

_____

_____

_____

Adjectives and Adverbs

Preview

WHAT ARE ADJECTIVES AND ADVERBS?

Adjectives give information about nouns (people, places, and things). Adverbs modify verbs, adjectives, and other adverbs.

adjectives before the noun   adverb

*He is a **tall, intelligent**, and **handsome** <u>man</u>. He works **quickly**.*

Adjectives have comparative forms (ending in *–er*) and superlative forms (ending in *–est*).

*He is **taller than** me. I am **shorter than** he is. He is **the tallest** person in the room.*

COMPARING

Write the names of three well-known people on the lines. Choose singers, actors, politicians, or athletes. Then compare them using the words below.

_____

_____

_____

    EXAMPLE: (richer) Eminem is richer than Drake.

1. (nicer) _____

_____

2. (the richest) _____

_____

3. (longer hair) _____

_____

4. (the oldest) _____

_____

5. (more popular) _____

_____

6. (the happiest) _____

_____

Reading and Listening

IDENTIFY ADJECTIVES AND ADVERBS

Read the paragraph and complete the sentences with the correct form of the adjectives or other words below. Make guesses and write your choices in the blanks. On the Companion Website, listen to an audio recording of the reading. You can correct your answers.

as   bad   common   cool   good   large   old   recent

1. What is the _____ youth subculture? **2.** Some argue that hipsters are the _____ group on most college campuses these days. **3.** Others say that metalheads are _____ than hipsters. **4.** Are emos and goths as popular _____ they were in the past? **5.** Which subculture is the _____? **6.** Which group has the _____ taste in fashion and music?

7. The word "hipster" is _____ than most people realize.

8. In the 1940s, a hipster was a person who was _____ than others.

9. Hipsters, also called "beatniks," listened to jazz, and some hipsters were _____ poets than others. **10.** Today, hipsters are not the same _____ they were in the past.

Adjectives: Forms and Usage

ADJECTIVE PLACEMENT

Adjectives appear *before* the nouns they modify or after linking verbs, such as *be*, *look*, *feel*, and *seem*.

before the noun

The **energetic young** *girl* was a wonderful dancer.

after the verb be

The *dancers* are **beautiful** and **passionate**.

ADJECTIVE FORM

Adjectives are always singular, even if the nouns they modify are plural.

Maria has ~~beautifuls browns~~ eyes. *(beautiful brown)*

COMPARATIVE AND SUPERLATIVE FORMS OF ADJECTIVES

		COMPARATIVE	SUPERLATIVE
Add –er or –est to one-syllable adjectives. When the adjective ends in a consonant-vowel-consonant, double the last letter.	short hot	short**er than** ho**tter than**	**the** short**est** the ho**ttest**
In two-syllable adjectives ending in a consonant + y, add –er or –est.	lazy	laz**ier than**	**the** laz**iest**
Add *more* or *most* to adjectives of two or more syllables.	modern	**more** modern **than**	**the most** modern
Irregular adjectives have special forms.	good bad little* far	**better than** **worse than** **less than** **farther than**	**the best** **the worst** **the least** **the farthest**

*(a small amount)

EQUALITY: AS ... AS/THE SAME AS

Both *as ... as* and *the same as* express equality.

*I am **as tall as** you.*
*My math mark is **the same as** yours.*

Sometimes one object is not as good as another.

*High heels are **not as comfortable as** running shoes.*

Adverbs: Forms and Usage

Adverbs give information about a verb. Most adverbs end in –*ly*. Some exceptions are the adverbs *fast, high, far, late, often,* and *soon,* which never end in –*ly*.

adjective	→	adverb	adjective	→	adverb
nice		nice**ly**	careful		careful**ly**
clear		clear**ly**	beautiful		beautiful**ly**

*Chopin played the piano **quickly**.*
(The adverb *quickly* describes the action of playing.)

COMPARATIVE AND SUPERLATIVE FORMS OF ADVERBS

	COMPARATIVE	SUPERLATIVE
Add *more* or *most* to adverbs that end in –*ly*.	**more quickly than**	**the most quickly**
Some adverbs have special forms and do not end in –*ly*.	**faster than** **more often than**	**the fastest** **the most often**

Practice

 For listening practice and to try additional exercises, visit the Companion Website.

TIP

Adjective or Noun?

A noun may act like an adjective when it modifies another noun. Remember that adjectives are singular.

The shirt costs fifty **dollars**.
(*Dollars* is a noun.)

It is a fifty-**dollar** shirt.
(*Dollar* acts as an adjective and modifies *shirt*.)

EXERCISE 1 ADJECTIVE FORM

In the italicized words below, identify and underline the noun. Then correct the error in the adjective form or word order. Write *C* beside the sentences that are correct.

EXAMPLE: People from the 1920s were the losts <u>generation</u>.   <u>lost</u>

1. In the 1920s, people watched *silents movies*.   _____

2. Young people listened to *jazz music*.   _____

3. Louis Armstrong was a *musician famous*.   _____

4. He played many *differents instruments*.   _____

5. He lived in a foster home for *three years and a half*.   _____

6. Armstrong travelled to *other countries*.   _____

7. He was not a *man tall and thin*.   _____

8. Sometimes he wore *coats long*.   _____

9. During the Great Depression, people could not buy *paper toilet*.   _____

10. Those *years* were very *difficults*.   _____

COMPARING WITH ADJECTIVES

Comparative: The skateboard is **slower than** the motorcycle.
                    The car is **more expensive than** the motorcycle.

Superlative: The skateboard is **the slowest** item in the group.
                    The car is **the most expensive** item in the group.

EXERCISE 2 COMPARATIVE AND SUPERLATIVE FORMS

Write the comparative and superlative forms of the following adjectives.

	COMPARATIVE FORM	SUPERLATIVE FORM
EXAMPLE: short	shorter than	the shortest
1. nice	_____	_____
2. good	_____	_____
3. natural	_____	_____
4. bad	_____	_____
5. happy	_____	_____
6. exciting	_____	_____
7. big	_____	_____
8. cute	_____	_____
9. useful	_____	_____

EXERCISE 3 CHOOSE ADJECTIVE FORMS

Write the comparative or superlative form of the adjectives in parentheses. Remember to use *than* in the comparative form and *the* in the superlative form.

EXAMPLE: This year, I am (happy) <u>happier than</u> I was last year.

1. I am (old) _____ child in my family.

2. My two brothers are (young) _____ I am.

3. Jordan is (young) _____ child in our family.

4. Jordan's marks are (good) _____ mine.

5. Jordan is (immature) _____ I am.

6. My middle brother, Lance, is (rebellious) _____ child in our family.

7. Lance is definitely (serious) _____ Jordan.

8. Jordan is (lazy) _____ person in our house. He never cleans anything.

9. These days, my parents are (relaxed) _____ they were when I was young.

TIP

Showing Equality

Both *as ... as* and *the same as* express equality.

My coat is **as nice as** Doug's coat.

EXERCISE 4 CHOOSE ADJECTIVE FORMS

Write the correct form of the adjectives below. You will need to use the comparative or superlative form or *as ... as*. There are key words in each sentence to help you. In the examples, the key words are in bold.

EXAMPLES: Equal   I am **as** (tall) <u>tall as</u> Lee.
         Comparative   *Lee is (nice)* <u>nicer</u> **than** *Angela.*
         Superlative   *Lee is* **the** *(old)* <u>oldest</u> *person in the room.*

1. What is the (good) _____ boy band? *Rolling Stone* magazine said that 'N Sync was the (great) _____ boy band in the last fifty years. A reviewer said that 'N Sync was (good) _____ than the Backstreet Boys. But 'N Sync was not as (good) _____ the Jackson 5. Michael Jackson was the (talented) _____ singer and dancer of the last century.

2. In the late 1990s, 'N Sync had two lead singers. At that time, JC Chasez was not as (popular) _____ Justin Timberlake. Chasez's voice was (bad) _____ than Timberlake's voice.

3. In 2002, Justin Timberlake made his first solo album. Today, Timberlake is (rich) _____ than Chasez. Justin Timberlake is the (creative) _____ singer from 'N Sync. He is also the (rich) _____ person from the band. Chasez's music career will probably not last as (long) _____ Timberlake's career. But Michael Jackson had one of the (long) _____ music careers in the industry.

TIP

Common Errors

Comparative and Superlative Forms
In the comparative form, never use *more* and *–er* to modify the same word.
In the superlative form, never use *most* and *–est* to modify the same word.

     Coffee is ~~more~~ **better** *than tea.*
     Green tea is the ~~most~~ **best** *drink.*

As ... as
When two items have equal value, place *as* after the adjective, not *than*.

            as
     Jared is as old ~~than~~ *I am.*

Each sentence below contains one error. Underline and correct the errors.

stronger
EXAMPLE: In the past, women were <u>strongest</u> than women today.

1. Some of greatest advances in women's rights happened during the 1920s.

2. Certain events were importants.

3. Conditions for women were worser in the 1920s than they are today.

4. During the "flapper" era, women wanted as much freedom than men had.

5. Nellie McClung was the greater activist in Canada.

6. McClung was more nicer than her sister.

7. In 1927, McClung was the bigger female critic of Canada's election laws.

8. Women wanted the same opportunities than men.

9. Today, women have most freedom than their grandmothers had.

TIP

Than, Then, and That

Do not confuse *than, then,* and *that*. Look at how each word is used.

Than is used when two items are compared.

*I am older **than** you are. You are shorter **than** I am.*

Then means "next" or "after that."

*We sold the company, and **then** we moved to Florida.*

That introduces a clause. *That* can also imply distance (as *this* implies closeness).

*Did you find the book **that** I gave you?*
*Lady Gaga recorded songs with **that** company.*

EXERCISE 6 IDENTIFY ERRORS WITH *THAN*, *THEN*, AND *THAT*

Underline and correct eight errors involving the usage of *than, then,* and *that*.

that
EXAMPLE: I love the music <u>than</u> is on your iPod.

1. I really love the MP3 player than my father bought me. It holds more songs that

   my old MP3 player. Recently, I downloaded many Beyoncé songs. I love the

   songs than she sings.

2. When I was a child, my father played the music of Destiny's Child. I thought than the singers had great harmony. Than, when I got older, I listened to Beyoncé Knowles.

3. Today, I think than Beyoncé has the best voice in the world. Her song "Single Ladies" is better then any other song. I believe than her music will last for a long time.

ADVERBS

An adverb modifies a verb, an adjective, or another adveb. Most adverbs end in –ly. But exceptions are adverbs such as *fast* and *often*, which never end in –ly.

*Allen walks **quickly**. He **often** exercises.*

EXERCISE 7 ADJECTIVES AND ADVERBS

Decide whether the italicized word is an adverb or an adjective. Add –ly when necessary. If no –ly is required, put an X in the space.

　　EXAMPLE: They talked loud **_ly_** about the Beat generation.

1. The Beat generation writers were very *popular*_____. They *often*_____ broke rules. They wrote poetry *different*_____ than anyone before them. They had *serious*_____ ideas. They wrote *serious*_____ about controversial topics.

2. Allen Ginsberg *successful*_____ completed the book *Howl* in 1957. Politicians thought that his book was *dangerous*_____. Ginsberg went to court to defend himself. Maybe the publicity was *useful*_____. The book became very *successful*_____.

3. Ginsberg lived *dangerous*_____. Sometimes, he had *extreme* _____ opinions. He *strong*_____ promoted a peaceful world view. The Beat writers influenced the hippie movement.

COMPARATIVE AND SUPERLATIVE FORMS OF ADVERBS

Most adverbs have two or more syllables. Use *more* and *the most* in comparative and superlative forms of adverbs.

*I work **the most slowly** in our team.*
*Jared types **more quickly than** I do.*

EXERCISE 8 ADJECTIVES AND ADVERBS

Write the comparative form of the following adjectives and adverbs.

EXAMPLE: The Silent Generation was (quiet) <u>quieter</u> than the previous generation.
Clara works (quietly) <u>more quietly</u> than I do.

1. The Silent Generation refers to children born during the Great Depression.
   They were (afraid) _____ than the previous generation.
   People lost jobs (easily) _____ than they had in the past.

2. In the 1920s, life was (easy) _____ than in the 1930s.
   People found jobs (quickly) _____ than they would during
   the Depression. In the 1920s, people lived (happily) _____
   than they would in the following decade.

3. Ruth Wade was born in 1934. She was (quiet) _____ than
   her older brother. Ruth studied (quietly) _____ than her
   brother did. He was (loud) _____ than his sister. He sang
   (loudly) _____ than Ruth did.

↺ UNIT Review

Answer the following questions. If you don't know an answer, go back and
review the appropriate section.

1. Correct the error in each sentence.
   a) Montreal is more larger than Ottawa.   _____
   b) The movie is not as good than the book.   _____
   c) What is the worse song in the world?   _____

2. Which two forms express that items have equal value?

   _____   _____

3. Write the comparative and superlative forms of the following adjectives.

	COMPARATIVE FORM	SUPERLATIVE FORM
EXAMPLE: short	shorter than	the shortest
a) good		
b) bad		
c) hot		
d) happy		
e) unusual		

Final Review

PART A

Write the comparative or superlative form of the following adjectives. Do not use *as ... as*.

EXAMPLE: My music is (good) <u>better</u> than your music.

Punk fans

1. Punk rock is (old) _____ than hip hop. The British claim that their punk movement was (important) _____ than American or Canadian punk.

2. In the 1970s, rock music was (soft) _____ than punk music. Punk musicians were the (angry) _____ _____ group of musicians at that time.

3. The Clash were (loud) _____ than the Beatles. According to many critics, punk singers were the (terrible) _____ singers in the world.

4. Johnny Rotten was a punk singer. He was (bad) _____ than other musicians. He was the (bad) _____ singer of all.

5. In 1977, punk rock fans were (dangerous) _____ than traditional rock fans. They were the (violent) _____ of all music fans.

PART B

Underline and correct the error in each sentence.

                                      than

EXAMPLE: Your shirt is newer <u>then</u> mine.

6. The first punk singers were not populars.

7. Johnny Rotten was the most craziest singer of the 1970s.

8. His songs weren't as good than Kurt Cobain's songs.

9. What is the worse type of music?

10. My guitar is more expensive that my piano.

PART C

Circle the letter of the best answer.

11. I don't have the same musical tastes ... you do.

a) than b) as c) then

12. There were more punk bands in Toronto ... there were in Calgary.

a) than b) that c) then

13. Punk bands wanted to be ... than soft rock bands.

a) louder b) loudest c) as loud

14. New punk music, or "pop punk," is ... than classic punk rock.

a) worser b) the worst c) worse

15. Are bands such as Green Day ... than the Sex Pistols?

a) more better b) better c) gooder

 **WRITING**

Write a paragraph, and compare your fashion style and musical taste to someone you know. You can compare yourself with a parent, a brother or sister, or a friend. Use at least three comparative forms and three superlative forms in your paragraph.

EXAMPLE: My brother's hair is longer than my hair.

_____

_____

_____

_____

_____

_____

_____

_____

_____

_____

_____

_____

_____

_____

UNIT 11

Spelling and Word Choice

Preview

DICTATION

Your teacher will read five sentences. Write each sentence. Then check your spelling.

1. _____
2. _____
3. _____
4. _____
5. _____

Spelling: Forms and Usage

ADDING PREFIXES AND SUFFIXES

A **prefix** is added to the beginning of a word in order to change the word's meaning. When you add a prefix to a word, keep the last letter of the prefix and the first letter of the main word.

mi**s** + **s**pell = mi**ss**pell   i**l** + **l**egal = i**ll**egal

A **suffix** is added to the ending of a word in order to change the word's meaning. When you add the suffix *–ly* to a word ending in *–l*, keep the original *l*. If the word ends in *–e*, keep the *–e*.

fina**l** + **l**y = fina**ll**y   sur**e** + **l**y = sur**el**y

WORDS ENDING IN –Y

In English, many words end in a consonant + *–y*. Do not write the following words with an *–ie* ending, unless you are using the plural form, which ends with *–ies*. For example, *activity* becomes *activities*.

activity	comedy	sociology	technology
captivity	economy	society	trophy

SPELLING OF TWO-PART WORDS

The following words sound as if they should be two separate words, but they are only one.

Words with *any*	anything, anyone, anybody, anywhere
Words with *some*	something, someone, somebody, somewhere, sometimes ("sometimes" meaning "occasionally")
Words with *every*	everything, everyone, everybody, everywhere

Another and **A Lot**

Another is always one word.   **Another** *gorilla escaped from the zoo.*
A lot is always two words.   **A lot** *of people are looking for the animal.*

COMMONLY MISSPELLED WORDS

Review the list of commonly misspelled words. (A more comprehensive list of misspelled words appears in *Avenues 1, Grammar Review Guide*.)

address	example	health	personality	school
apartment	exercise	human	practice	success
business	family	interesting	problem	technology
career	finally	medicine	questioned	visit
course	future	ninth	really	with
environment	government	park	restaurant	which

Commonly Confused Words: Forms and Usage

SOME COMMONLY CONFUSED WORDS

always	a situation exists at all times	You are **always** late.
still	a past situation continues to exist	I am **still** waiting for you!
again	a past action is repeated	The computer crashed **again**.
live	(verb) exist (adjective) not prerecorded	I want to **live** with you. We should go to listen to some **live** music.
life	(noun) existence	I have a great **life**.
leave	(verb) exit; go away	We will **leave** in ten minutes.
learn	discover new information	I want to **learn** how to cook.
teach	instruct or give knowledge to	My mother will **teach** me how to cook.
to	indicates direction or movement, or is part of an infinitive	I want **to** go **to** Florida.
too	also or very	Florida is **too** hot in the summer. It is hot in Texas, **too**.
two	the number after one	There are **two** whales in the marine park.
fun	pleasant/a pleasant time	My trip to Italy was **fun**.
funny	humorous	Robert is so **funny**! He makes me laugh.

Continued

| watch
look at
look for | view something that moves
view something that is immobile
search for | We will **watch** a movie tonight.
I want to **looked at** the paintings.
I can't find my keys. I will **look for** them. |

REALLY AND *VERY*

Really and *very* mean "extremely."

Put **very** before adjectives.
Put **really** before adjectives and verbs.

*The food is **very** good.*
*She is **really** nice.*
*I **really** like that movie.*

SOME, NO, AND *ANY*

The following rules apply to all words containing *some, no,* or *any,* such as *somewhere, someone, anything, nowhere,* and *nobody.*

Use **some** in affirmative sentences.
Use **no** in negative sentences.
Use **any*** in negative sentences that
    include the word "not."
Use **some** or **any** in questions.

*There is **some**thing in my soup.*
*I need **no** help.*

*No, there is**n't any**thing in your soup.*
*Do you want **some** soup? Do you want **any** bread?*

* Note that *any* also means "it doesn't matter which."   *Eat **any** fruit that you want.*

Practice

 For additional exercises about spelling and word choice, visit the Companion Website.

EXERCISE 1 SPELLING

Correct the spelling errors in the following words. Write *C* next to the words that are spelled correctly.

EXAMPLE: carreer _____career_____

1.	futur	_____	**11.** appartement	_____
2.	family	_____	**12.** cours	_____
3.	restaurent	_____	**13.** whit	_____
4.	scool	_____	**14.** exemple	_____
5.	visite	_____	**15.** exercise	_____
6.	technologie	_____	**16.** wich	_____
7.	generaly	_____	**17.** ilegal	_____
8.	interresting	_____	**18.** probleme	_____
9.	activitie	_____	**19.** beautifull	_____
10.	medicine	_____	**20.** healt	_____

EXERCISE 2 IDENTIFY SPELLING ERRORS

Correct twelve spelling errors in the underlined words. Write *C* over three correct words.

EXAMPLE: I go to zoos <u>sometime</u>. [written above: *sometimes*]

1. Do you care about the <u>environment</u>? <u>Alot</u> of cities have marine <u>parcs</u> with dolphins and whales. Defenders say that the animals have <u>every thing</u> that they need. However, marine animals have a high death rate in <u>captivitie</u>. <u>Sometime</u> in marine parks, one well-known whale is <u>realy</u> ten or eleven different whales. After a whale dies, <u>an other</u> whale replaces it and has the same name.

2. Marineland is in Niagara Falls, Ontario, and it has several Orca whales. In the wild, an Orca has a long lifespan and can live as long as <u>humains</u> do. But in marine parks, the <u>ordinary</u> lifespan of an Orca is just eleven years. The animals are not in good <u>healt</u>. Some activists want marine parks to close. However, the Canadian <u>governement</u> is very quiet about the issue. <u>Every body</u> knows the <u>probleme</u> is serious. I will never <u>visit</u> a park that has whales.

EXERCISE 3 *STILL, ALWAYS, AND AGAIN*

Fill in the blanks with *still*, *always*, or *again*. You can review the meanings of the terms on page 114.

EXAMPLE: It is May, but it is _still_ cold outside. Why isn't the spring coming?

1. It is midnight, and I can't sleep. I am _____ awake.

2. My neighbour, Sebastian, has a dog. In the morning, the dog barked for about an hour. It was quiet during the day, but now it is barking _____.

3. Every night the dog barks, and it _____ keeps me awake.

4. I called the police last month. Should I call the police _____?

5. In the past, I _____ treated my neighbours with respect, and I never made noise late at night.

6. Now it is 1 a.m. and that crazy dog is _____ barking.

EXERCISE 4 WORD CHOICE

Fill in the blanks with one of the words in parentheses.

EXAMPLE: (two / to / too) Lee went _to_ a zoo with _two_ friends.

1. (life / live / leave) I want to improve my quality of _____ . If I want to _____ longer, I should exercise. I want to _____ for eighty years. It will be hard to _____ my meat-eating lifestyle, but I will try. Most vegetarians _____ longer than people who choose to eat meat. People who _____ their meat-eating lifestyle can reduce their risk of cancer by fifty percent.

2. (to / two / too) Most of my friends are _____ attached to the taste of meat. I enjoy eating meat _____, but I want to change my diet. I gave my friends _____ reasons to become vegetarians. First, they need _____ lose weight. Meat production is bad for the environment, _____.

3. (learn / teach) My neighbours are vegetarians. Every week, they _____ me how to cook vegetarian meals. I _____ about beans and vegetables. In the future, I will _____ my children to cook. They will _____ healthy eating habits.

4. (fun / funny) Every weekend, I have _____ with my friends. We go downtown, and we do something that is _____. Last week, we rented a really _____ old movie called *The Hangover*. The actors were so _____ that we could not stop laughing!

EXERCISE 5 WORD CHOICE

Underline and correct the errors in spelling and word choice. Write *C* beside the sentences that are correct.

                              too
EXAMPLE: Factory farming is <u>to</u> dangerous.

1. Jason very wants to fight for animal rights.

2. In his opinion, the conditions in meat factories are to crowded and to unhealthy.

3. Most animals on factory farms have very short lives.

4. I very don't understand why people eat meat.

5. Most cows leave in crowded conditions, and they have no room to move.

TIP

Really or *Very*

Be careful. Don't put *very* before a verb.

    really
    I ~~very~~ like
    that movie.

6. The cows are not content. They definitely do not have funny.

7. Anna and I very don't like to eat meat.

8. I am very sad about the situation.

SOME, NO, AND ANY

Use *some* in affirmative sentences and *no* in negative sentences. Use *any* in sentences that contain "not."

> We have **some** bread but we have **no** butter. We do**n't** have **any** jam.

In questions, you can use *some* or *any*.

> Do we have **some** bread? Do we need **any** butter?

EXERCISE 6 *SOME, ANY, OR NO*

1. Fill in the blanks with *some, any,* or *no.* In some cases, there is more than one choice.

Jared: I cooked _____ tofu for dinner. I don't

want _____ red meat.

Kara: Well, I would like _____ steak. Are there

_____ steaks in the fridge?

Jared: No. There are _____ steaks. In fact, you

won't find _____ meat in the house.

You should not eat _____ red meat. It

is bad for your health.

2. Fill in the blanks with *somebody, nobody,* or *anybody.*

Kara: I just went to the grocery store, but it was closed. I could not see

_____.

Jared: It is 9 p.m. The store closed an hour ago, so _____ is there now.

Kara: Is another store open?

Jared: I don't know. You will have to ask _____ else.

Kara: I don't know _____ who is as stubborn as you are.

3. Fill in the blanks with *something, nothing,* or *anything.*

Jared: I'm going to cook you _____ that will make you forget meat.

Kara: I don't want _____ that has tofu in it. I hate tofu.

Jared: You're acting silly. I'll make you _____ delicious.

Kara: I won't eat _____ except a pork chop. If there is no meat

in the house, then I will eat _____ for dinner.

NO AND ANY

To give *any* a negative meaning, you must add *not* to the sentence. *No* has a negative meaning on its own. The following pairs of sentences have the same negative meaning.

I **don't** have **any** time.   I have **no** time.

I **don't** want **anything** to eat.   I want **nothing** to eat.

EXERCISE 7 *NO AND ANY*

PART A

Change *any* to *no*. Remember to remove the negative verb forms.

EXAMPLE: I don't want any coffee. _I want no coffee._____

1. I didn't receive any gifts. _____

2. We don't know anybody. _____

3. There aren't any girls here. _____

4. He doesn't have any money. _____

PART B

Change *no* to *any*. Remember to add the negative verb forms.

EXAMPLE: He likes nobody. _He doesn't like anybody._____

5. She has no friends. _____

6. We need no help. _____

7. I want nothing. _____

8. He has no free time. _____

WATCH, LOOK, LISTEN

Do not confuse watch, look, and listen. Review the meanings.

We **watch** something that is moving.

*He is **watching** television.*

We **look at** something that is immobile.

*They are **looking at** photos.*

We **look for** (or *search for*) an object that is lost.

*She is **looking for** her keys.*

We **listen to** something that makes sound.

*He is **listening to** music.*

TIP

Watch TV

You do not listen to TV shows and movies. You **watch** them.

Shane is ***watching*** *TV.*

EXERCISE 8 *WATCH, LOOK, AND LISTEN*

Underline and correct the errors involving word choice. You might need to add the missing prepositions *to*, *for*, or *at*.

EXAMPLE: I am <u>listening to</u> a movie.   _watching_

1.   I listen the radio every Saturday morning when I drive to work.   _____

2.   What TV show do you listen most often?   _____

3.   I like to look artwork by Picasso.   _____

4.   I can't find the remote control. Could you help me look it?   _____

5.   Why are you looking the sky? What is so interesting?   _____

6.   When the teacher speaks, you should listen him.   _____

7.   Did you lose your wallet? We need to look it.   _____

8.   We should listen some music to help us relax.   _____

9.   Tomorrow we are going to the art museum to look some art.   _____

10. Tonight, I will listen a movie.   _____

↻ UNIT   Review

Answer the following questions. If you don't know an answer, go back and review the appropriate section.

1.   Underline three correctly spelled words. Cross out the incorrectly spelled words.

famelly   which   scool   thougth   with   writing

2.   Underline the appropriate words in parentheses.

a) My brother is (to / too) lazy.

b) He (listens to / watches) television all day. He (very / really) likes police shows.

c) He (still / again / always) (lives / leaves) with our mother, but he doesn't like it. He (always / still / again) complains.

d) We will play a game and have (funny / fun) tonight.

e) Jason doesn't listen to (nobody / anybody).

Need more practice? Visit the Companion Website and try additional exercises.

Final Review

PART A

Correct the spelling errors in the following words. Write C next to the words that are spelled correctly.

1. familly   _____
2. futur   _____
3. cours   _____
4. finally   _____
5. exercice   _____

6. exemple   _____
7. visit   _____
8. activitie   _____
9. probleme   _____
10. restaurent   _____

PART B

Underline the appropriate word in parentheses. Note that X means "nothing."

1. Some people (always / again) indulge their pets. Ten years ago, when I first met Caroline, I noticed that she spent (to / too / two) much money on her dog. At that time, she didn't buy (anything / nothing / something) special for herself, but she would buy expensive food for her dog. A month ago, I met Caroline (still / again / always), and I noticed that she (still / again) spends a lot on her pet. She bought her dog an expensive coat.

2. Caroline has an apartment nearby. We have a lot of (fun / funny) together. She tells interesting stories, so I love to listen (at / to / X) her. Also, we (really / very) love movies. Two weeks ago, we rented a comedy. The movie was so (fun / funny) that we laughed for a long time. After the movie was over, we chose (an other / another) film. A good documentary can (learn / teach) us many things about our planet.

3. Last week, Caroline and I (watched / listened) a documentary called *Food Inc.* The movie (learned / taught) me many things. I didn't know (nothing / anything) about the food industry. I could not look (to / at) some of the scenes.

4. In the past, I ate (a lot / alot) of red meat. Now, I take care of my health. I eat (no / any) red meat. When I shop for food, I look (for / on / to) chicken or pork. I want to (leave / live) for a long time. I know that I (really / very) need to eat well.

 **WRITING**   On a separate piece of paper, write a paragraph about a movie that you like. What did you learn from it? After you finish writing, review your spelling and word choice.

Sentences and Punctuation

Preview

WHAT IS A COMPLETE SENTENCE?

A complete sentence has a subject and a verb, and it expresses a complete idea. It begins with a capital letter and ends with a period (.), question mark (?), or exclamation mark (!).

Did you hear me? I can't leave. It's too cold outside!

IDENTIFY ERRORS

Correct ten errors in sentence structure or punctuation.

Last friday night, an accident. Brigitte and i were downtown, it was cold and icy. Brigitte fell and hurt herself when she crossed market street. She hurt her leg, and she wanted see her doctor. It was late, her doctors office was closed. We took a taxi to the hospital. The emergency room was full. Too many people! We waited for twelve hours to see a doctor.

Sentences: Forms and Usage

SENTENCES

A sentence can have more than one subject or verb.

One subject and one verb:	*Martin likes* music.
Two subjects:	*Martin* and *Tanya live* together.
Two verbs:	*Tanya sings* and *writes* songs.

To give your writing more variety, you can join two complete sentences with a **coordinating conjunction**.

Use **and** to join two complete ideas.	*I am single, **and** I am happy.*
Use **but** to contrast two ideas.	*I am single, **but** Joan is married.*
Use **or** to offer an alternative.	*I'll eat salad, **or** I'll eat fries.*
Use **so** to indicate an effect.	*I live alone, **so** I pay a lot of rent.*

COMMON SENTENCE ERRORS

Fragments

A fragment is an incomplete sentence. It is missing a subject, a verb, or a main clause. To correct a fragment, add the missing part, or join it to another sentence. Review the fragments and the corrections.

No subject:	*Travels with her husband.*
No verb:	*First, dangerous drivers.*
No main clause:	*Because* he needed money.*

*A subordinator such as *because* introduces a secondary idea. Make sure that your sentence also has a primary idea.

Possible Corrections

Add a subject:	***Clara** travels with her husband.*
Add a verb:	*First, **consider** dangerous drivers.*
Add a main clause:	***Terrel found a job** because he needed money.*

Run-Ons

A run-on occurs when two complete ideas are joined incorrectly with a comma. Review the run-on and the possible corrections.

Incorrect	*Roy paints, he also writes books.*
Possible Corrections	*Roy paints, **and** he also writes books.*
	*Roy paints. **He** also writes books.*

Punctuation and Capitalization: Forms and Usage

APOSTROPHES (')

Apostrophes in Contractions

Use an apostrophe to join a subject and verb together.

***We're** late. **There's** nothing to eat.*

Also use an apostrophe to join an auxiliary with *not*.

*I **can't** come. They **aren't** very friendly.*

Apostrophes to Show Possession

You can add *apostrophe –s ('s)* to nouns to indicate possession.

*Michael is the child of Jane. He is **Jane's** child.*

If the noun is plural, put the apostrophe after the –s.

The **girls'** toys are in the basement.

If the noun has an irregular plural form, add –'s.

The **men's** room is down the hall.

COMMAS (,) AND PERIODS (.)

Use commas (,)

- To separate three or more words in a series (Put the comma before the final *and*.)

  She is kind, considerate, and gentle.

- In quotations, after an introductory phrase

  She said, "I feel alone."

- Around interrupting phrases that give additional information about the subject

  Kevin, a student at Victoria College, doesn't know how to drive.

Use periods (.)

- At the end of a complete sentence
- After the following titles: *Ms.   Mrs.   Mr.   Dr.*

CAPITALIZATION

Always capitalize the following:

- The pronoun "I" and the first word of every sentence

  The car that **I** drive needs some repairs.

- The days of the week, the months, and holidays

  Friday   **J**une 3   **L**abour **D**ay

- The names of specific places, such as buildings, streets, parks, public squares, lakes, rivers, cities, provinces, and countries

  Spring **S**treet   **L**ake **E**rie   **H**alifax, **N**ova **S**cotia

- The names of languages, nationalities, tribes, races, and religions

  German   **M**ohawk   **B**uddhist

- The titles of specific individuals

  General **D**allaire   **P**rime **M**inister Brown   **M**rs. **S**mith

- The titles of specific courses

  Physics 201   **F**rench 100   **B**eginner's **S**panish

- The important words in titles of literary or artistic works

  Source Code   *One Tree Hill*   *Bad Romance*

Practice

EXERCISE 1   IDENTIFYING FRAGMENTS AND RUN-ONS

Write *C* next to complete sentences. Write *F* next to fragments, and write *RO* next to run-ons.

> **EXAMPLE:** Many nations fascist dictators.   F

1. A king or queen governed England and France. ____

2. Democratic governments in Ancient Greece. ____

3. Men could vote, women could not vote. ____

4. Because men owned property. ____

5. Women fought for the right to vote, they did not succeed for many years. ____

6. Most Canadian provinces gave women the vote in 1919. ____

7. The first province, Manitoba. ____

8. Some provincial governments did not agree with the new law. ____

9. Quebec, for example. ____

10. In Quebec, women received the right to vote in 1940. ____

WRITING COMPLETE VERBS

Make sure that your verbs and infinitives are complete. In general, if a verb is followed by another verb, use the infinitive form (*to* + base form) of the second verb. If the verb is followed by a noun, it isn't necessary to use *to*.

| infinitive | verb + noun |
| We really need <u>to talk</u>. | We <u>need money</u>. |

EXERCISE 2 **CORRECTING SENTENCE ERRORS**

Identify and correct the errors in the sentences below. Some of the sentences are missing a subject or a verb, some are joined incorrectly, and some have an incomplete infinitive.

                   are
EXAMPLE: Some people ∧ very funny.

1. Martin Neufeld wanted have a successful acting

   career.

2. He studied drama at Dawson College because are

   good acting coaches at that school.

3. In 2004, no work in Montreal's film industry.

4. Martin Neufeld wanted to work, so came up with

   a great idea.

5. He went to Montreal's Old Port. Because many tourists go there.

6. He wrote "Free Hugs" on a sign, many people stopped.

7. Neufeld wanted help others.

8. In other cities, some students decided give free hugs.

9. Many people live alone, they need some human contact.

10. Human affection and laughter very important.

APOSTROPHES (')

If the noun is singular, put the apostrophe **before** the –s. If the noun is plural, put the apostrophe **after** the –s. If the noun has an irregular plural form, add –'s.

Singular:	***Sandra's*** *daughter is cute.*
Plural:	*The **boys'** shoes are in the hall.*
Irregular Plural:	*The **children's** bedrooms are messy.*

EXERCISE 3 APOSTROPHES TO SHOW POSSESSION

Write the possessive form of the following phrases.

EXAMPLE: the brother of Paul _____Paul's brother_____

1. the coat of the girl _____

2. the coats of the girls _____

3. the family of Anne _____

4. the life of the artist _____

5. the lives of the artists _____

6. the purse of the woman _____

7. the restroom of the women _____

EXERCISE 4 ADD APOSTROPHES

Write the possessive form of the nouns below. The nouns may require an apostrophe or apostrophe + –s.

EXAMPLE: The hospital **_'s_** waiting room is full.

1. Canada____ health-care system is highly

respected around the world.

2. Simon____ mother works at the Montreal

Children____ Hospital.

3. Andrea Ng saves many people____ lives.

4. Her boss ____ health isn't very good.

5. The patients ____ beds are comfortable.

6. The head nurse ____ cousin is a hospital administrator.

7. Where is the men ____ room?

8. There are many medical students, and the students ____ books are expensive.

TIP

Common Apostrophe Errors

Don't use apostrophes before the final –s of a verb or a plural noun.

      wants   **towns**

Mr. Lee want's to visit several town's.

In negative contractions, the apostrophe replaces the missing –o in *not*.
(Exception: *will + not = won't*)

      doesn't

He does'nt have any money.

EXERCISE 5 ADD APOSTROPHES

Underline ten words that require an apostrophe in the sentences below. Then add the apostrophes.

                    sister's

EXAMPLE: My <u>sisters</u> husband works in Vancouver.

1. Vancouvers in an earthquake zone, but most people dont worry about it.

2. One time, my sisters dogs predicted an earthquake. Both dogs tails started to shake, and they ran in circles. Usually, theyre very quiet animals. Normally, they dont bark.

3. When were older, my sister and I plan to travel to South America together. Shell take time off work, and Im going to ask for a long vacation. Were not going to bring the dogs.

TIP

Commas and Periods

Do not separate a subject and verb with a comma.

The new mall, has many great stores.

Use periods (.)

- At the end of a complete sentence
- After the following titles: *Ms.   Mrs.   Mr.   Dr.*

EXERCISE 6 ADD PUNCTUATION

Underline and correct one punctuation error in each of the sentences below.

      EXAMPLE: The <u>museums</u> artwork is very beautiful.   _____museum's_____

1. Many artists paintings are unique.   _____

2. Marcel Dzama, is a Canadian painter from Winnipeg.   _____

3. He usually paint's people.   _____

4. Many of his painting's appear in museums.   _____

5. He works, in a large studio.   _____

6. His paintings are unique because theyre humorous.   _____

7. He creates soldiers fragile monsters, and bears.   _____

8. Mr Beck commissioned an artwork for his album cover.   _____

9. Macy Sullivan an accountant, wants to buy a painting.   _____

10. She often says "I love Dzama's artwork."   _____

TIP

Capitalization

Capitalize the names of specific places and titles. If you do not mention a specific name, no capitals are necessary.

*There is a busy <u>street</u> near my home. It is called **P**orter **S**treet.*
*I live near a <u>river</u>. My house is close to **E**lbow **R**iver.*

EXERCISE 7 ADD CAPITAL LETTERS

Add twenty missing capital letters to the following sentences. You can review the capitalization rules on page 124.

                                                F

      EXAMPLE: Lourdes wanted to learn french.

1. Lourdes is from mexico, and she speaks spanish.

2. She is living with a canadian girl in Vancouver.

3. Next summer, they will rent a house on cedar avenue. It is a very busy street.

4. Lourdes is learning english at redwood school.

5. She goes to school from monday to thursday, but she gets fridays off.

6. On weekends, she works at a restaurant called food barn.

7. Right now, she is reading a magazine called *nylon*.

8. Lourdes is interested in buddhism, and she has several books on the subject.

9. Lourdes and i hope to rent a cabin near a lake. We want to rent one on echo lake.

10. In august, mr. Rice will rent his cabin to us.

⟲ UNIT Review

Answer the following questions. If you don't know an answer, go back and review the appropriate section.

1. Correct the following sentences. Ensure that each sentence is complete.

   a) We made a poster, it was very large.

   b) Our poster was very big. Because we wanted many people to see it.

   c) We tried put many pictures on the poster.

2. Add the necessary punctuation and capital letters to the following sentences.

   a) martin and i hope to learn spanish were going to mexico in february.

   b) hes good at learning languages.

   c) were going to leave on valentines day.

Need more practice?
Visit the Companion Website
and try additional exercises.

Final Review

PART A

Identify and correct five sentence errors. Look for fragments, run-ons, and incomplete verbs.

                             to
EXAMPLE: Carol wanted_buy a CD.

Lady Gaga studied piano in New York, and she hoped have a successful singing career. In 2007, she made a recording. With some friends. She wanted become famous, and she decided wear unusual clothing and masks. Many people bought her CDs, she became an international star.

PART B

Make twenty corrections to the sentences below. Add sixteen capital letters and four apostrophes.

                    A   's
EXAMPLE: Last <u>april</u>, <u>Adelas</u> mother became very ill.

1. Maya is learning english and french at university. Last july, she moved to drolet street with her two children. Maya is brazilian.

2. She rented the apartment from mr. Grey. He owns a store called The world of crafts. The apartments front window faces the street.

3. Mayas brother lives near the Museum of fine arts. He visits the museum every friday.

4. Maya doesnt see her brother very often because theyre very busy.

5. In july, they plan to visit moon lake. They will swim in the lake with their venezuelan friends.

WRITING On a separate piece of paper, write a paragraph about the place where you live. What is the address? What are the nearest main streets? What are advantages and disadvantages of your current location? After you finish writing, check that you have complete sentences and correct punctuation.

Editing Practice and Tense Review

Editing Practice

Practise editing student writing. The exercises contain a variety of errors.

EXERCISE 1 COMPATIBLE ROOMMATES

Correct fifteen errors in the student paragraph, not including the example. An editing symbol appears above each error. To understand the meaning of each symbol, look at the Editing Guide on the inside back cover of this book.

       English
    C   WC

Today, in my english class, I met Vincent and Angela. Vincent have eighteen years

            SP   SV   SING   WO

old, and he haves one sister. He work every weekends at a station service. Vincent

              PL   O

and I have the sames attitudes. We don't smoke, we like cook, and we pay our

                        VT   C   SV

bills. So we are compatible. Angela is born on july 14th. She don't cook, and she

WC   SP

very likes to be alone, so we are not compatible. But I was happy to talk whit

                  WO   C

her because she is a person very nice. Next monday, I want to speak with

                                             SP

Angela and Vincent again because they are friendly poeple.

EXERCISE 2 NATURE

Correct ten errors in the student paragraph, not including the example. An editing symbol appears above each error. To understand the meaning of each symbol, look at the Editing Guide on the inside back cover of this book.

        X   VT

I love ~~the~~ nature. Every day, I am walking in a forest near my house. When I was

                 SP   O

young, my family haved a cottage. I really loved go to the country house because

          WF   SP

I could doing many things. For exemple, I walked in the woods, and I swam in the

SP   P   RO

lac. I did'nt like video games, I preferred to spend time outdoors. In the future,

O   ⌢

I going to live near a forest. I don't want to move to an other province. I will stay

here and buy a cottage near my town.

EXERCISE 3 THE SILENT GENERATION

Correct fifteen errors in the student paragraph, not including the example. An editing symbol appears above each error.

                       DS

The Silent Generation it was people who were born bewtween 1925 and 1945.

     WC   WC   WC   WC

In these days, life was more difficult then now. Some men went at war. There have

                            DS   SING

no seatbelts in the cars, so driving it was risky. Women's lives were difficults. Most

         VT   WF   WF

women can't worked outside the home. Couples wouldn't divorce even if theirs

                 X   WF   F

problems were severe. The divorce wasn't frequently. Also, large families. People

    VT   WC

was having many children. Life was not as easy as it is for us generation. It was

         WC

very hard to live at this moment in time.

EXERCISE 4 TRADITIONS AND CELEBRATIONS

Underline and correct twelve errors in the following student paragraphs. (There are six errors in each paragraph.)

1. In each countries, people have specials traditions. Sometimes, they have celebrations for remember a war or an important person. Also, in many cultures, people celebrate birthdays. For example, I am born on may 14th. Every years, I receive gifts from my parents.

2. I remember my last birthday very well. When I had eighteen years old, I went at a restaurant with my friends. After, we played different games card. Then, when it was very late, we went to club in Montreal. I didn't arrived home until the morning. It was the most best day of my life.

Tense Review

AVOID FAULTY TENSE SHIFTS

If you start to describe a past event, be careful not to shift tenses unless the time frame really changes. In the example below, the first two sentences are part of a past tense story, while the third sentence is a generalization.

> When I **worked** as a waitress, I **received** some very good tips. Almost everyone **gave** me a fifteen percent gratuity. Nowadays, so many people **expect** tips that many people no longer **understand** tipping etiquette.

A **faulty tense** shift occurs when your verb tenses change for no logical reason.

> rested
> We went to Mexico, and we ~~rest~~ on the beach every day.

TIP

Would and *Could*

When you tell a story about a past event, use *would* instead of *will* and *could* instead of *can*.

> would   could not
> In the 1950s, people ~~will~~ only tip in restaurants. Gas station attendants ~~cannot~~ ask for tips.

EXERCISE 5 TENSE INCONSISTENCY

Underline and correct eight faulty tense shifts in the following paragraphs.

> worked
> **EXAMPLE:** When Simon was sixteen years old, he ~~works~~ as a bellhop in a very fancy hotel.

1. Every day, Simon greeted the hotel guests and bring their luggage to their rooms. One day, a woman entered the hotel. She was wearing a white fur coat and a long dress. Everyone looked at her because she's wearing evening clothes in the middle of the morning.

2. The woman had twelve pieces of luggage. Simon told the woman that he will help her. He carefully loaded the bags onto his trolley, and then he pushes the trolley into the elevator. When he arrives at the woman's room, he carried in the twelve bags. Some of the bags are very heavy. The woman asked Simon to arrange the baggage around the room carefully.

3. That night, while the woman was taking a shower, a thief enters the room. He took some jewellery, and then he closes the door quietly.

EXERCISE 6 "HOW" QUESTIONS

Add the missing word to each question. Choose from the following:

| far | long | many | much | often | old |

> **EXAMPLE:** How _much_ is that coat? Does it cost more than $15?

1. How _____ is the movie: two or three hours?

2. How _____ are you? Are you eighteen years old?

3. How _____ do you travel: once or twice a year?

4. How _____ people are in the lineup? Are there a lot of people?

5. How _____ is Fredericton? Is it more than 200 kilometres from here?

6. How _____ was Jake when he moved away? Was he sixteen years old?

7. How _____ did you live in Nova Scotia? Did you live there for one year or two years?

8. How _____ is that car? Does it cost more than $10,000?

9. How _____ does the power go out? Is it a weekly occurrence?

EXERCISE 7 QUESTIONS

Students wrote questions for Gerard Jones, the author of "Killing Monsters" on page 93 in *Avenues 1: English Skills*. Each question has an error. Correct each question.

                     do

    EXAMPLE: Where ^ you live?

1. When you started to write comic books?

2. Why your stories was violent?

3. In the past, what do your favourite story was?

4. What did you before you became a writer?

5. Where you are living now?

6. How much long is your book?

7. What your mother is doing right now?

8. Why your books have so much violence?

9. In the future, do you will write more books?

EXERCISE 8 VERB TENSE REVIEW

Fill in the blanks with the correct tense of the verbs in parentheses. Then write a yes/no question and a negative statement. For help, you can refer to the tenses section in *Avenues 1 Grammar Review Guide*.

    EXAMPLE: Rory (be) _is_ from Calgary. (simple present)
                 Question Form: _Is Rory from Calgary?_
                 Negative Form: _Rory isn't from Calgary._

1. Rory (speak) _____ four languages. (simple present)

   Question: _____

   Negative: _____

2. She (sing) _____ right now. (present progressive)

   Question: _____

   Negative: _____

3. They (move) _____ to Canada last year. (simple past)

Question: _____

Negative: _____

4. They (be) _____ busy yesterday. (simple past)

Question: _____

Negative: _____

5. Rory (be) _____ in a good mood last week. (simple past)

Question: _____

Negative: _____

6. She (be) _____ twenty years old next summer. (future)

Question: _____

Negative: _____

EXERCISE 9 EIGHT KEY RULES

In this exercise, errors represent eight major grammar problems. Each error is in bold. Correct the error. Then write a rule for each error.

1. Caroline **don't** travel. Every summer she **stay** home and **work**.

Rule: _____

See Unit 2, page 13, for more information about the simple present.

2. **They have** a lot of reasons why people celebrate. **It have** good reasons and

bad reasons. For example, every year, to celebrate a high school graduation,

it have a party.

Rule: _____

See Unit 2, page 16, for more information about *there is* and *there are*.

3. When I was young, I **was go** to Europe with my family. Every year, I **was visiting**

France.

Rule: _____

See Unit 4, page 36, for more information about the simple past.

4. I went **in** Europe with my family. Every summer, we go **at** many places.

Rule: _____

See Unit 8, page 86, for more information about prepositions.

5. Most people like **a holidays**. But some people don't go to **a ceremonies** such

   as **a weddings** or **a funerals**.

   Rule: _____

   See Unit 5, page 54, for more information about articles.

6. I **can't gave** all of the reasons. In the future, I **will taught** my children about

   Christmas.

   Rule: _____

   See Unit 9, page 92, for more information about modals.

7. **Youngs** adults travel to many **differents** places.

   Rule: _____

   See Unit 10, page 104, for more information about adjectives.

8. People love to **travel, it's** a passion for them. They visit other **countries, they**

   learn many things.

   Rule: _____

   See Unit 12, page 123, for more information about sentences.

Irregular Verb List

The following list has three columns.

- The **base form** appears in dictionaries. It has no special verb ending.
  - EXAMPLE: You didn't <u>study</u>.

- Use the **simple past** form with the simple past tense. (See Unit 4.)
  - EXAMPLE: We <u>flew</u> to England.

- Use the **past participle** form in perfect and passive structures. (See Appendix 4, Point 6.)
  - EXAMPLE: They have <u>been</u> together since 2004.

BASE FORM	SIMPLE PAST	PAST PARTICIPLE
be	was/were	been
beat	beat	beat/beaten
become	became	become
begin	began	begun
bend	bent	bent
bet	bet	bet
bite	bit	bitten
bleed	bled	bled
blow	blew	blown
break	broke	broken
bring	brought	brought
build	built	built
buy	bought	bought
catch	caught	caught
choose	chose	chosen
come	came	come
cost	cost	cost
cut	cut	cut
deal	dealt	dealt
dig	dug	dug
do	did	done
draw	drew	drawn

BASE FORM	SIMPLE PAST	PAST PARTICIPLE
drink	drank	drunk
drive	drove	driven
eat	ate	eaten
fall	fell	fallen
feed	fed	fed
feel	felt	felt
fight	fought	fought
find	found	found
fly	flew	flown
forget	forgot	forgotten
forgive	forgave	forgiven
freeze	froze	frozen
get	got	got/gotten
give	gave	given
go	went	gone
grow	grew	grown
hang	hung	hung
have	had	had
hear	heard	heard
hide	hid	hidden
hit	hit	hit
hold	held	held

BASE FORM	SIMPLE PAST	PAST PARTICIPLE
hurt	hurt	hurt
keep	kept	kept
kneel	knelt	knelt
know	knew	known
lay	laid	laid
lead	led	led
leave	left	left
lend	lent	lent
let	let	let
lie[1]	lay	lain
lose	lost	lost
make	made	made
mean	meant	meant
meet	met	met
mistake	mistook	mistaken
pay	paid	paid
put	put	put
prove	proved	proved/proven
quit	quit	quit
read[2]	read	read
ride	rode	ridden
ring	rang	rung
rise	rose	risen
run	ran	run
say	said	said
see	saw	seen
sell	sold	sold
send	sent	sent
set	set	set
shake	shook	shaken
shoot	shot	shot
show	showed	shown
shrink	shrank	shrunk
shut	shut	shut

BASE FORM	SIMPLE PAST	PAST PARTICIPLE
sing	sang	sung
sink	sank	sunk
sit	sat	sat
sleep	slept	slept
slide	slid	slid
speak	spoke	spoken
speed	sped	sped
spend	spent	spent
spin	spun	spun
split	split	split
spread	spread	spread
stand	stood	stood
steal	stole	stolen
stick	stuck	stuck
sting	stung	stung
stink	stank	stunk
strike	struck	struck
swear	swore	sworn
sweep	swept	swept
swim	swam	swum
swing	swung	swung
take	took	taken
teach	taught	taught
tear	tore	torn
tell	told	told
think	thought	thought
throw	threw	thrown
understand	understood	understood
upset	upset	upset
wake	woke	woken
wear	wore	worn
win	won	won
withdraw	withdrew	withdrawn
write	wrote	written

1   *Lie* means "to rest or lie down on a sofa or bed." When *lie* means "tell a false statement," it is a regular verb:
    lie, lied, lied.
2   The present form of *read* is pronounced "reed." The simple past and past participle forms are pronounced "red."

Parts of Speech

PARTS OF SPEECH	DEFINITION	EXAMPLE
adjective	• adds information about the noun	small, hot, beautiful, green ...
adverb	• adds information about the verb • expresses time, place and frequency	easily, nicely, quickly, quietly ... sometimes, usually, often, never ...

conjunction	• connects two parts of a sentence
	  –**Coordinating**: connects two ideas of equal importance
	  –**Subordinating**: connects a subordinate (or secondary) idea to the main idea
		and, but, so, or
		
		after, although, because, unless ...

determiner	• identifies or determines if the noun is specific or general	a, an, the, this, that, these, those, each, every, much, many, some
noun (common)	• a person, place or thing	**Singular**: woman, cat, person ... **Plural**: women, cats, people ...
noun (proper)	• a specific person, place or thing Proper nouns are capitalized.	Jamaica, Doctor Reed, Samson, Lake Ontario, Golden Gate Bridge, Calgary ...
preposition	• shows a relationship between words (source, direction, location, etc.)	above, at, behind, below, for, from, of, to ...
pronoun	• replaces the noun	he, she, it, us, ours, themselves ...
verb	• expresses an action or state	drive, talk, think, walk

PRACTICE

Label each word with one of the following terms.

adjective	conjunction	noun	pronoun
adverb	determiner	preposition	verb

EXAMPLE: blue   _adjective_

1. herself _____
2. and _____
3. human _____
4. carry _____
5. below _____
6. often _____

7. into _____
8. they _____
9. discuss _____
10. children _____
11. quickly _____
12. Dr. Smith _____

Idioms

An idiomatic expression has a different meaning than the words suggest.
Review the idiomatic expressions and their meanings.

Behaviour

bite the hand that feeds you	—be unfriendly to someone who helps you
butter someone up	—flatter someone
clear the air	—remove worry or suspicion by talking about something openly
pick a fight	—deliberately start a fight
put your foot down	—show your authority over someone
see eye to eye	—agree with someone
think outside the box	—think creatively

Health

be hard of hearing	—be unable to hear well
binge drinking	—drinking too much alcohol in a short period of time
feel blue	—feel depressed
pull through	—survive or recover from a sickness
recharge your batteries	—leave a stressful activity to rest and replenish your energy
touch and go	—have an uncertain outcome (after an operation, a person's condition can be "touch and go")
up and about	—if you are up and about, you recovered from an illness

Lifestyle

be a couch potato	—watch too much television; be inactive
drag your feet	—procrastinate
go the extra mile	—do more than is expected
pull your weight	—do your fair share of the work

Shopping

go on a shopping spree	—spend a lot of money shopping
it's a steal	—it's a great price
live beyond your means	—spend more than you earn
need retail therapy	—believe that buying items will make you feel better
shop till you drop	—shop until you are completely tired
window-shop	—to look in store windows but not buy anything

Travel

backseat driver	—car passenger who gives unwanted advice to the driver
have itchy feet	—feel constant desire to see new places
have road rage	—to react aggressively to a driving incident
hit the road	—start the trip; begin a journey
travel lightly	—bring very little luggage

Frequently Asked Questions

1. When do I add –s or –es to verbs?

Add –s to present tense verbs that follow a third-person singular subject. The term "third-person singular" refers to **one** person, place or thing—except *you* and *I*.

Exception: change *have* to *has*

One person	*Every morning, Valerie <u>walks</u> to work.*
One thing	*The problem <u>deserves</u> careful consideration.*
One place	*The pool room <u>has</u> many tables.*

Don't add –s to:

▪ Verbs that follow *you, we, I,* or *they*	*They <u>walk</u> to work.*
▪ Past tense verbs	*She <u>walked</u> to work.*
▪ Future tense verbs	*He <u>will walk</u> to work.*
▪ Modals	*She <u>can walk</u> to work.*

2. What is the "base form" of the verb?

The **base form** is the verb form that you find in dictionaries. It has no special ending.

eat   go   sleep   watch

3. What is an auxiliary?

An **auxiliary** is a helping verb. It appears before another verb and helps to indicate tense or mood.

auxiliary
*She **will** <u>visit</u> us next year.*

Auxiliary verbs are added to many question and negative forms.

auxiliary
***Do** you <u>want</u> more information?*

auxiliary
***Did** the town <u>clean</u> the water system?*

auxiliary
*We **do** not <u>work</u> together.*

A special type of auxiliary is called a **modal**. Modals indicate concepts such as desire, obligation, or ability. Examples include *can, could, should, would, may,* and *might*.

modal auxiliary
*Veronica **can** <u>speak</u> Spanish.*

4. What is the difference between *do, does,* and *did*?

Do, **does**, and **did** are forms of the verb *to do*.

He <u>does</u> his homework. I <u>do</u> the dishes.

Do, **does**, and **did** are also auxiliaries that are added to question and negative verb forms.

▪ Add **do** to simple present tense questions and negative forms.

| *You work a lot.* | ***Do** you work a lot?* | *You **do**n't work a lot.* |

▪ Add **does** to simple present tense question and negative forms *when the subject is third-person singular*.

| *She works a lot.* | ***Does** she work a lot?* | *She **does**n't work a lot.* |

▪ Add **did** to simple past tense question and negative forms.

| *Yesterday they studied.* | ***Did** they study?* | *They **did**n't study.* |

5. Do some questions have no auxiliary?

Yes. When *who* and *what* ask about the **subject** of a question, no auxiliary is needed.

subject
***Simon** lives with Angela.*
↑
***Who** lives with Simon?*

subject
***The car** needs a new engine.*
↑
***What** needs a new engine?*

6. Can I put *have* or *has* before past tense verbs?

No. When you write in the past tense, simply use the simple past form of the verb.

Present tense	**Past tense**
We go out.	*We **went** out.*
The doctor works hard.	*The doctor **worked** hard.*
She has many problems.	*She **had** many problems.*

However, there is a verb tense that you may learn more about in a future course. It is called the **present perfect** tense and it is formed with ***have*** or ***has*** **+ the past participle**. (The past participle is in the third column of irregular verb lists. For example, the past participle of *go* is *gone*. The past participle of regular verbs is simply the *–ed* form of the verb.)

Examples of the present perfect tense:

*Many astronauts **have explored** outer space. John Glenn **has been** to space twice.*

The present perfect tense is used in two ways.

1. One or more past actions occurred at an indefinite past time. Key words include *once, twice, many times, already.*

   *Ariel **has been** to Mexico three times.*
   (We don't know exactly when she went to Mexico.)

2. An action started in the past and continues to the present. Key words include *since, for,* and *ever.*

   *Yann **has lived** in Canada since 1994.*
   (He came to Canada in 1994 and he still lives here.)

Don't confuse the present perfect tense with the simple past tense. When you tell a story about a past event, use the simple past.

                                learned
When I was young, I ~~have learned~~ to play the violin.

7. What is the passive voice?

Sometimes in sentences, the subject does not do the action. The subject receives the action. Notice the difference between the active and the passive voice.

Active Voice

*Italian workers **make** shoes.*
(The subject is active. The workers do the action.)

Passive Voice

*Shoes **are made** in Italy (by Italian workers).*
(The subject is passive. The shoes do not do the action. They are affected by the action.)

To form the passive, use the verb *be* + the past participle. Review the examples.

VERB TENSE	ACTIVE	PASSIVE
simple present	We **admire** athletes.	Athletes **are admired** (by the public).
simple past	The boss **hired** Jacob.	Jacob **was hired** (by the boss).
future	He **will buy** the company.	The company **will be bought** (by him).

Grammar Log

Grammar Log

Each time a writing assignment is returned to you, identify one or two repeated errors and add them to your Grammar Log. Then, consult the Grammar Log before you hand in writing assignments in order to avoid making the same errors. For each type of grammar error, you could do the following:

1. Identify the assignment and write down the type of error.
2. In your own words, write a rule about the error.
3. Include an example from your writing assignment.

EXAMPLE: _Paragraph_ (Oct. 2nd) Subject-Verb Agreement
    In the simple present, add –s to verbs that follow _she_.

                    bites
    She often _bite_ her nails when she is nervous.

_____

_____

_____

_____

_____

_____

_____

_____

_____

_____

_____

_____

_____

_____

_____

_____

_____

_____

INDEX

PHOTO CREDITS

ALAMY
p. 45 (left): Alexander Sandvoss
p. 58 (right): Image Source
p. 76: Adrian Lyon
p. 77: Robert Fried
p. 79 (right): David Crausby
p. 81: redsnapper
p. 82: David Coll Blanco
p. 85 (top): redsnapper
p. 88: ICP
p. 89 (top): redsnapper
p. 110: The Art Archive

BIGSTOCK
p. 16 (left): archidea
p. 16 (left): billberryphotography
p. 27 (top, right): rgbspace
p. 30 (centre, left): AlienCat
p. 30 (top, right): keeweeboy
p. 47 (bottom, centre): Daniela Michel
p. 47 (bottom, centre): JR Trice
p. 47 (bottom, right): Michale Flippo
p. 86: eileen meyer
p. 109 (top, left): Edward Wallace
p. 125 (top, left): Steve Woods
p. 125 (bottom, right): Jon Pullinger
p. 127: Christophe Nicolas Konfortion

COURTESY OF AUTHOR
p. 23 (centre, centre)
p. 23 (centre, right)
p. 26 (bottom, left)

CP IMAGES
p. 100 (bottom)

ISTOCKPHOTO
p. 5 (bottom, right): attator
p. 18: Linda Yolanda
p. 19: Diego Cervo
p. 20: Muhammet Göktas
p. 36 (left): Mona Plougmann
p. 38: S. Prada
p. 52 (top, left): gchutka
p. 89 (right): susaro
p. 93: bobbieo
p. 128: ROMA-OSLO
p. 130 (left): Arpad Benedek

SHUTTERSTOCK
p. 1: Tania Zbrodko
p. 2: Zoran Karapancev

p. 4 (top, left): mikeledray
p. 4 (centre, left): tkemot
p. 4 (bottom, left): Robert Kneschke
p. 4 (top, right): Liudmila P. Sundikova
p. 4 (centre, right): Maksim Shmeljov
p. 4 (bottom, right): StockLite
p. 5 (top, left): Yuri Arcurs
p. 5 (top, centre): Rui Vale de Sousa
p. 5 (top, right): Alex Mit
p. 7: Nadiia Gerbish
p. 9: AYAKOVLEV.COM
p. 11 (top): Tania Zbrodko
p. 11 (bottom): Cindy Hughes
p. 12: RUDVI
p. 13: ZanyZeus
p. 15: Leah-Anne Thompson
p. 16 (left): stocksnapp
p. 16 (left): design56
p. 16 (left): Garsya
p. 16 (left): Jaimie Duplass
p. 16 (left): oksana2010
p. 16 (left): EuToch
p. 16 (left): Shiva
p. 17: Eric Isselée
p. 21: Feng Yu
p. 22 (top): RUDVI
p. 22 (top, left): Eric Isselée
p. 23 (top): Pavzyuk Svitlana
p. 23 (centre, left): Kurhan
p. 23 (bottom, left): ImageryMajestic
p. 23 (bottom, centre): Fotocrisis
p. 23 (bottom, right): Supri Suharjoto
p. 24: Evgeny Tyzhinov
p. 26 (bottom, right): James Peragine
p. 27 (top, left): Konstantins Visnevskis
p. 27 (centre, left): Vlad Mereuta
p. 27 (centre, right): Yuri Arcurs
p. 28 (left): Val Thoermer
p. 28 (centre, left): FXQuadro
p. 28 (centre, right): Gelpi
p. 28 (right): Paul Matthew
p. 29 (left): Morgan Lane
p. 29 (right): lakeemotion
p. 30 (top, left): Luke Schmidt
p. 30 (centre, right): Yuri Arcurs
p. 31: Gina Smith
p. 33 (top): Pavzyuk Svitlana

p. 33 (centre): Maxim Petrichuk
p. 35: Andrey Yurlov
p. 36 (right): Timothy R. Nichols
p. 39 (left): Jaroslaw Grudzinski
p. 39 (left): Dusan Po
p. 39 (left): Phant
p. 39 (left): Feng Yu
p. 39 (left): Ragnarock
p. 39 (left): Monica Butnaru
p. 39 (left): Picsfive
p. 41: Warren Goldswain
p. 43 (top): Ben Haslam
p. 43 (bottom): Motmot
p. 45 (top): Andrey Yurlov
p. 47 (top): Kapu
p. 47 (bottom, left): Elnur
p. 47 (bottom, left): Kert
p. 48: Jacek Chabraszewski
p. 50 (top, left): Katrina Brown
p. 50 (top, left): Melissa Schalke
p. 52 (bottom, left): Evangelos
p. 53 (top, left): Digital Genetics
p. 53 (top, right): A1Stock
p. 53 (bottom, right): Racheal Grazias
p. 54: arindambanerjee
p. 55: dmitrieva
p. 58 (top): Kapu
p. 59 (top): Supri Suharjoto
p. 59 (bottom): Michael D. Brown
p. 59 (bottom): Digital Genetics
p. 62: Dariush M.
p. 63 (top): Alperium
p. 63 (bottom): Andrea Danti
p. 66 (centre): Strejman
p. 66 (bottom): Sergey Peterman
p. 67: Heizel
p. 68 (top): Supri Suharjoto
p. 69: Pete Saloutos
p. 70 (top): kavram
p. 70 (bottom): Vuk Vukmirovic
p. 71: Ackab Photography
p. 73: Bobby Deal
p. 74 (top): Amy Walters
p. 74 (bottom): Gina Smith
p. 75: jbor
p. 79 (top): kavram
p. 83 (top, left): Osipovfoto
p. 83 (top, left): Igor Leonov
p. 83 (bottom, left): zentilia
p. 83 (top, centre): Utekhina Anna
p. 83 (bottom, centre): Alex Staroseltsev

p. 83 (top, right): Al Mueller
p. 83 (bottom, right): Tony Campbell
p. 85 (bottom): Ambient Ideas
p. 91 (top): olly
p. 92: woodygraphs
p. 95: Dgrilla
p. 97: Kamila Panasiuk
p. 98: Henrik Winther Andersen
p. 99: willmetts
p. 100 (top): olly
p. 102: Refat
p. 103: Hiku, Inc.
p. 105 (centre, left): akva
p. 105 (bottom, left): Andrew Buckin
p. 105 (bottom, centre): Margo Harrison
p. 105 (bottom, right): Maksim Toome
p. 106: Apollofoto
p. 107: Helga Esteb
p. 108: Mayer George Vladimirovich
p. 109 (bottom, right): Yuri Arcurs
p. 111 (top): Refat
p. 111 (left): Iakov Filimonov
p. 113: J van der Wolf
p. 116 (top, left): Stephen Coburn
p. 116 (bottom, right): Eric Isselée
p. 117: tepic
p. 118: OLJ Studio
p. 119 (left): Ivan Josifovic
p. 119 (left, centre): fotum
p. 119 (right, centre): Bernd Jürgens
p. 119 (right): IKO
p. 121 (top): J van der Wolf
p. 121 (bottom): Elena Rostunova
p. 122 (top): Helder Almeida
p. 122 (left): Nick Martucci
p. 126: iofoto
p. 129: auremar
p. 130 (top): Helder Almeida
pp. 131, 137: Rob Marmion